For Hal,

Ethics Consultation

whose easy charm & practical wisdom inspire me

Warmest regards

Hal

To Hal —
a throbbing sex thing!

Ethics Consultation
A Practical Guide

John La Puma, MD
Consultant in Clinical Ethics
Department of Internal Medicine
Lutheran General Hospital
Park Ridge, Illinois

David Schiedermayer, MD
Department of Medicine
Medical College of Wisconsin
Milwaukee, Wisconsin

JONES AND BARTLETT PUBLISHERS
Boston   London

Editorial, Sales, and Customer Service Offices
Jones and Bartlett Publishers
One Exeter Plaza
Boston, MA 02116
1-800-832-0034
1-617-859-3900

Jones and Bartlett Publishers International
PO Box 1498
London W6 7RS
England

Library of Congress Cataloging-in-Publication Data
La Puma, John.
   Ethics consultation : a practical guide / John La Puma, David
Schiedermayer.
      p.   cm.
   Includes bibliographical references and index.
   ISBN 0-86720-797-3
   1. Medical ethics — Practice. 2. Medical consultation.
I. Schiedermayer, David. II. Title.
   [DNLM: 1. Ethics, Medical. 2. Consultants. 3. Referral and
Consultation. W 50 L317e 1994]
   R725.5.L36 1994
   174'.2 — dc20
   DNLM/DLC
   for Library of Congress   93-28098
                                                     CIP

Photo credits: p. 65: Courtesy of Larrie Sarff, Associate Professor of Pediatrics, Children's Hospital of Wisconsin; pp. 37, 99, 140, 146, 187: Courtesy of John Easton, Director of Public Affairs, The University of Chicago; p. 1: Courtesy of Peggy DeVita, Boulder, Colorado; pp. 132, 168: Courtesy of Jim King, Director of Public Relations, Froedtert Memorial Lutheran Hospital; p. 156: Courtesy of Children's Hospital, Boston.

Printed in the United States of America
97 96 95 94 93   10 9 8 7 6 5 4 3 2 1

To our patients and their families

▎ Contents

Preface

Ethics consultation should seek to improve patient care. Both practicing physicians, we have learned that case solving is related to more than just the patient's medical prognosis. Cases often turn on other discrete social, cultural, religious, economic, and personal elements.

One of us (John La Puma) is a faculty member in an ethics center and a hospital consultant; the other (David Schiedermayer) is a clinician–educator and an ethics committee member. Together, we have performed about 700 formal ethics consultations. When we began consulting, we looked for a book about the process and technique of clinical ethics consultation. None was available, so we have attempted to write one that will help others interested in this work. While our efforts to describe the process are only an initial exploration, we have tried to write about what we have experienced. As a result, this text is focused primarily on the clinical model of ethics consultation — in the hospital, clinic, nursing home, and office. We hope the basic observations presented herein will prove practical and helpful.

The field of medical ethics is replete with general books that offer many theories and conflicting approaches. Readers looking for such a book will probably be disappointed by this one; this is a book about a specific consultation method with actual patient care examples. We explain how consultations are performed, briefly telling some patients' stories. In this book we describe the work of the consultant at the patient's side, the skills and roles of the consultant, and the potential outcomes in different cases. We also address the professional, institutional, personal, and financial issues faced by ethics consultants, as well as the relationships of ethics consultants with ethics committees and other institutional committees.

We offer a few cited references for each chapter and the Appendix, and a longer annotated bibliography with references largely from peer-reviewed journals and relevant to the content of each chapter, as well as all of the books we know of that have been published on ethics consultation.

While an effort has been made to use pronouns that reflect the clinical arena (where ethics consultants, doctors, nurses, and patients are both "he" and "she"), one pronoun, "he" or "she," may be used for those involved in the cases. The reader should know we mean "he or she" in these cases.

The success of this endeavor will be gauged by whether those interested in doing consultation — practicing physicians, ethics committee members, nurses, attorneys, philosophers, students, house officers, medical educators — are able to learn here about its practical aspects. It is our goal to show how ethics consultation can lead to better patient care.

Acknowledgments

We are indebted for the personal and intellectual contributions of a large number of friends and colleagues. We received excellent training from Mark Siegler and the faculty of the Center for Clinical Medical Ethics at the University of Chicago. During our training, Steve Miles modeled the role of the ethics consultant. We are also grateful for Mark's mentoring.

Bill Winslade and Stephen Toulmin helped shape the idea for this book when all that existed was the idea. Stephen also helped us to formulate our definition of a "clinician" and our very brief explanation of modern medical casuistry. Felicia Miedema, Diane Arathuzik, Anne Kibrick, and Rachel Spector provided helpful insight into the nurse's role as an ethics consultant. Art Derse, John Fletcher, Bud Hammes, Carl Junkerman, Edmund Pelligrino, E. Rush Priest, and Bob Veatch reviewed this book carefully, critically, and generously. Their suggestions helped, and we thank them for their time, expertise, and wisdom. We would also like to say thank you to Joseph Burns, Vice President and Publisher of Jones and Bartlett Publishers, for believing in the book from the beginning. His early support and encouragement are very much appreciated.

Bill Arnold, Liz Gordon, Robyn Shapiro, Harold Shafter, Jim Byrd, and Leighton Smith gave us the opportunities to perform ethics consultation in our institutions and provided sponsorship and support for ethics consultation.

We would also like to acknowledge our families: Larry and Audrey Schiedermayer, Arnie and Mabe Grummer, Kim, Jon, Dan, and Ellie. Linda Ferrara, Salvatore and Linda and Joan La Puma, John and Clare Corre, Chris, Lorelei, Michael, Elizabeth, Peter, and Rosemary. We care about ethics in large measure because of the early encouragement, teaching, and support our families gave us.

Finally, the Lutheran General Hospital, the Lutheran General Medical Group, and the Medical College of Wisconsin provided us with continuing salary support and enough freedom to write this book. For this, and for our colleagues in these special places, we are grateful.

John La Puma
David Schiedermayer

1
Case Consultation

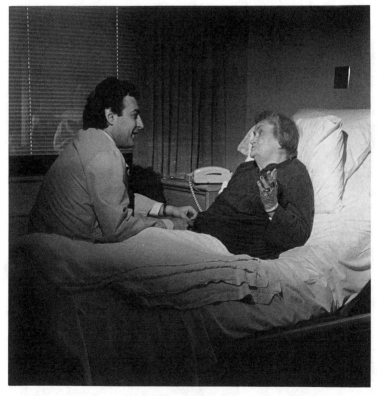

Talking with patients is the clinical approach to ethics consultation.

Consultants seek to learn all the relevant details of a case, to clarify treatment goals, and to outline a variety of ethically acceptable actions. In providing consultation services, a consultant identifies, analyzes, and helps to resolve ethical problems using expertise and skills. The consultant's training and skills fit the process of case consultation (see Table 1–1).

Sometimes, cases start like the one that follows.

Hector Garcia is a 45-year-old man who developed liver failure from alcoholic cirrhosis. The request for consultation came from an intensive care unit fellow, who described the scene: "This man is dying. He has encephalopathy and can't talk with us. His family wants all treatment continued. They seem like a nice enough family, but they won't even let us have a "No Code" order. We've been playing along, but enough is enough. We've given him 40 units of packed red blood cells, 6 donor packs of platelets, and 75 units of fresh frozen plasma. In spite of all this, his coagulation profile is worsening. When can we stop?"

The consultant asked the fellow for more details: Was there an advance directive? What were the patient's wishes before he became encephalopathic? Are there any other family members?

The fellow replied, "There was no advance directive. We didn't have a chance to talk with the patient before this, and the last team said that he really wasn't able to talk very well. The patient is divorced, and only his father and mother and siblings visit."

The consultant considered whether a phone consultation would suffice. After all, he could imagine Mr. Garcia on the ventilator, eyes jaundiced, abdomen protuberant with ascites. He could picture the family, insisting on all treatment against reasonable hope. He could even envision the tired fellow and the medical students standing by Mr. Garcia's bedside, going over the lab values. Instead of handling the case by phone, however, he went to see the patient.

In this chapter, the process of consultation will be outlined, and the importance of personally seeing patients will be discussed.

THE REQUEST FOR CONSULTATION

The invitation to see the patient is a voluntary, discretionary solicitation. Requests for consultation usually come from attending physicians for their hospitalized patients, but the requests may also originate with patients, families, nurses, house officers, students, other health professionals, hospital attorneys, or administrators. In their wish to serve all members of the health care community, some ethics consultants accept requests from persons other than the attending physician. While this view is understandable and appears egalitarian, the consultation risks failure without the assent of the attending physician. For the consultation to be effective, the attending physician must at least agree with the request, regardless of who raises the idea of consultation, who initially contacts the consultant, who signs the consultation request sheet, or who telephones the consultant's office or answering service.

Several reasons exist for this insistence on a formal invitation from the attending physician. First, it is at the least discourteous and quite possibly arrogant to consult on a patient's case without the attending's permission. Second, the attending's permission and solicitation facilitates the consideration of the consultant's advice. Third, the attending physician is ethically, legally, and medically responsible for the overall management of the patient. Fourth,

Table 1–1   *Process of Case Consultation*

Beginning the consultation

  Identify issues

  Determine urgency

  Understand question

Preparing to see the patient

  Speak with nurses and family

  Review key literature

  Read medical record

  Keep clinical notes

Seeing the patient

  Observe

  Gather own data

  Establish relationship

  Begin the conversation

    Introduce oneself
    Allow patient to speak without interruption
    Ask open-ended questions

  Examine the patient

    Perform mental status exam
    Examine key organ systems, as appropriate

Conducting family meetings

  Facilitate communication

  Avoid large meetings

Preparing an ethical analysis

  Identify goals and values

  Develop framework

Talking with the requesting physician

Writing a report

  Address question asked

  Provide four recommendations

  Provide references

Following up

  See patient next day, and prn

patients and families often directly (and properly) ask the attending for expert opinions from medical consultants in other fields. When patients and families ask for special help, the attending nearly always agrees to a consultation. Fifth, even if another member of the medical team wants an ethics consultation, the attending physician does not always want or need such a consultation.

Especially in the latter case, some nonphysician members of the health care team may want to have direct access to the ethics consultant. A well-defined mechanism should exist that allows other caregivers (for example, nurses) to discuss cases with the consultant. The JCAHO has mandated nursing access to ethics committees. The requesting nurse's clinical standing as the patient's primary caregiver almost always results in the attending physician's agreement to a consultation. In certain settings, such as home health care or long-term care facilities, nurses may function independently as a primary case manager and thus may call the consultant directly. If a formal consultation is desired, the attending physician of record should assent to the consultation.

Occasionally, the request for consultation centers on the behavior of the attending physician. For example, if a staff nurse believes that a physician is acting unethically and that a patient is being harmed, the nurse may call the consultant directly. The consultant can give the nurse several options: to discuss the problem directly with the physician; to appeal the problem to a supervisor or a hospital administrator, who could speak with the physician; or to contact the department chair or the medical director of the particular hospital unit and explain the nature of the problem. These options encourage action to prevent harm to the patient but also acknowledge that an actual ethics consultation cannot occur unless there is an invitation from the attending physician.

Suppose, however, that the problem is blatant — for example, a nurse tells the ethics consultant that a urologic surgeon has admitted a close relative to the intensive care unit and insists on writing all orders, or a physician tells the consultant that a colleague is operating on a patient while under the influence of drugs or alcohol. Here, the consultant can intervene by helping the nurse and doctor contact the physician assistance committee, department chair, hospital chief executive officer, or medical staff president. In this setting, the consultant provides assistance without providing an official consultation. More appropriate channels already exist to address these problems of professional practice, and those channels should be utilized by the individuals involved. The consultant cannot hope to survive the role of an uninvited moral troubleshooter.

The consultant should almost never refuse a request for consultation from an attending physician. While the consultant may decline to play certain roles that more properly belong to others, it is often difficult for the consultant to tell precisely what is required until the patient is seen. The ethics consultant should be willing to get involved in each case, at least until the actual ethical problems emerge. As the cases in the Appendix demonstrate, sometimes the ethical problems that are unmasked by the consultation differ from the original question(s) of the requesting physician.

BEGINNING THE CONSULTATION

After the request has been received, and usually before doing anything else, the consultant speaks with the primary attending physician and the resident in institutions where house officers make many key decisions. The consultant seeks to clarify the requesting physician's goals of consultation. Some of the first questions the consultant should ask are: What is the central clinical problem? What has prompted the request for consultation? It is helpful to develop a list of core questions to begin to identify the ethical issues in the case.

In this initial conversation, the consultant attempts to obtain as much information as possible; for example, how long the patient and physician have been acquainted, how well the physician knows the patient and family, whether the attending physician (or a previous physician) discussed the problem at hand, what the patient has said and when he or she said it, and the nature of the patient's major disease processes and mental status. The consultant may ask if other relevant consultants have seen the patient, such as a neurologist if the question concerns the withholding of life-sustaining treatment in a neurologically impaired patient. The consultant also tries to discover if there is any disagreement. The consultant should ask the patient's name and location and if the patient and family know that the consultant has been asked to see them.

The ethics consultant can also use this conversation to discover the urgency of the consultation. The consultant rarely does a full consultation by telephone. Consultants should avoid giving advice without seeing the patient, unless it is a clinical emergency. If it is late at night and the requesting physician thinks the patient cannot wait until the next day, the ethics consultant must see the patient then. It is much better to see a patient emergently than to learn at morning report or in the doctors' lounge that a bad decision was made in the middle of the night.

The consultant should try to understand and answer the physician's question even when it does not require formal analysis. For example, a requesting physician may call an ethics consultant to ask whether antibiotics should be withdrawn before pressors are stopped in a patient for whom the decision has already been made that the withdrawal of life-sustaining treatment is appropriate. This sort of question — the order of withdrawal, or improving the humaneness of withdrawal — is important even if it does not require sustained or formal ethical analysis. Similarly, when a difficult-to-start intravenous (IV) line falls out, replacing the IV or ensuring the availability of IV access becomes an "ethical" issue, which should be regarded as an immediate, practical question with underlying moral implications.

When the question concerns other issues that do not involve ethics, for example, concerns about a second opinion, the consultant should still be interested and available. Several approaches may be taken to such cases. The consultant may empathize, may refer the requester to other more appropriate medical, legal, or administrative sources, or may simply see the patient.

Sometimes, a full consultation is not desired or desirable; for example, the requester might be a specialist not in charge of the case, the primary attending might not want an ethics consultation, the patient might be about to return home, or the family might be tired of new consultants. In these cases, the ethics consultant could offer to do a consultation "just for education." If there are special financial constraints on care, and the patient or family is worried about the cost of additional consultation, the consultant could offer to adjust the fee, together with the adjustments of other practitioners.

"Curbside" consultations come from requesting physicians who approach the consultant in places like the parking lot, mail room, cafeteria, hallway, and elevator. Like most consultants, the clinical ethicist does curbside consultations reluctantly, as by definition, only a few data are available about any given case. In these instances, the consultant often tries to restrict his or her comments — for example, by providing only current hospital policy about tube feeding withdrawal — and can ask to see the patient officially. The consultant should avoid giving paternal or uninformed ethical opinions. The consultant should never provide detailed advice without seeing the patient.

PREPARING TO SEE THE PATIENT

Patient Background

In rare circumstances, the consultant may see a patient emergently. Emergencies can occur when the patient is undergoing a procedure, the physicians or family are keenly worried, or a critical family member or health professional is on an especially tight schedule.

In a nonemergent situation, however, the consultant can speak with the primary nurse to learn the details of the case. If appropriate, the consultant can ask the nurse when the patient is most alert and able to talk, whether and when the patient's family or friends visit, and how the patient and visitors seem to get along. The consultant can ask whether family and friends seem reliable and well intentioned. The consultant can also ask the nurse's perception of the problem and how it could be resolved. The nurse should be able to provide observations about patient–family interactions, staff sentiment, and communication to the consulting physicians in the case.

Other consultants may have valuable information to offer about the patient's condition. The consultant can try to speak with them, and occasionally attempts to arrange to see the patient along with them. House staff and medical students may serve as the patient's primary physicians in university teaching hospitals. The feelings and thoughts of resident and student physicians are often different from those of attending physicians, and the consultant should try to elicit these concerns. Like nurses, house staff and students often have important and undervalued perceptions of the ethical problems at hand.

After the consultant has spoken with the attending, the nurses, and the house staff, it is time to see the patient. In most cases, there is not a pressing need to review the medical literature relevant to the case beforehand. If the consultant is unfamiliar with the clinical problem, however, reading review articles or standard texts or calling a colleague in the field for a primer is both necessary and useful. On occasion, the consultant may want to bring to the initial visit certain articles, books, statutes, policies, or studies concerning the specific area of ethical difficulty in question. Usually, however, the ethics consultant is better able to assess what needs to be read and reviewed after seeing the patient.

Increasingly, ethics consultants are asked to see outpatients, home care patients, and those in long-term care facilities. These patients' cases may raise different types of ethical issues from inpatient cases. For example, the hospice care of a patient may not involve the common hospital issue of tube feeding (discouraged by most hospice policies) but, rather, the home use of antibiotics for comfort. The consultant can prepare to see these patients just as he or she prepares to see inpatients: by speaking with the requesting physician, home health care nurses and therapists, and family members and friends, and by reviewing the pertinent literature, laws, or health care regulations.

Patient Records

Before seeing the patient, the consultant should review the medical records. These documents present a great deal of important information in a logical, chronologic, and familiar order. The review gives the consultant an immediate sense of the patient's history and saves the other clinicians in the case valuable time, as they do not have to relate the entire story. The medical record also provides a multidisciplinary perspective, because it contains many views (for example, from nursing, social services, physicians, any pre-hospital team, and nursing home personnel). When carefully read, the records will often reveal reasons for the differing views on a case, and sometimes will show that highly emotional disagreements exist.

The consultant then begins to make his or her own notes, detailing important events in the patient's course. When the patient has been hospitalized for only a few days, the consultant can easily read the chart from front to back. This perspective enables him or her to see the flow of the case, especially in the progress notes, and may allow the consultant to conceptualize the case as a recorded whole, from the DNR order sticker on the inside of the front cover to the family's phone number on a Post-it note in the back. Examples of the consultant's initial notes include the following:

- Admission date
- Admitting diagnosis
- Attending physician
- Other consultants
- Current medical problems
- Medications
- Family members and phone numbers
- Laboratory data

Some charts, of course, are very long and detailed, and the consultant may have difficulty knowing where to begin. If the chart is voluminous or if it includes records from previous hospitalizations, the consultant might start with the progress notes, looking for an off-service note or a recent consultation. If the consultant is working in a university teaching hospital, he or she can look for a complete history and physical performed by a medical student or house officer. In a private practice setting, such as a community hospital, the same information is usually available from a summary note or the admitting physician's history and physical. Then the consultant can read back through the progress notes to find where the "ethics consult" (and possibly the consultant's name) is first mentioned.

Next, the consultant can read the doctors' orders sheets. Orders to limit or discontinue treatment, for example, can be directly compared with progress notes of the same day. The consultant reviews the laboratory and radiographic results, looking for major findings important to the case. When reading the nurses' notes, the consultant can look for a patient's interactions with the staff and for direct patient and family quotations — phrases common in nurses' notes but, unfortunately, relatively rare in physicians' notes. The consultant can also determine the patient's insurance status (especially important when the attending physician or nurse report financial problems), any utilization review concerns, or a potential economic conflict of interest.

Records from the emergency department, ambulance team, and operating room staff are often overlooked but may contain important data, unavailable elsewhere, which may strongly influence the outcome of a case. For example, in one case, a psychiatrist judged a patient with large cell cancer of the lung with metastases to the brain to be incompetent to make decisions about her health care "because of organic neoplastic disease." The CT scan performed and recorded in the emergency department, however, showed cerebellar, not cerebral, metastases. Careful evaluation of decision-making capacity confirmed that the patient could indeed decide where she wanted to go when she left the hospital.

The consultant's own notes should reflect the relative importance of these data to the ethical problem. At the very least, the consultant can list date of admission, admitting diagnosis, admitting physician, consulting physicians, medical problems and working diagnoses, current and recently discontinued medications, relevant family members with phone numbers, and relevant and pending laboratory findings, such as the HIV antibody status in an intravenous drug abuser or the peripheral white count and differential in a patient with leukemia.

SEEING THE PATIENT

After considering any initial discussions and reviewing the hospital records, the ethics consultant is ready to see the patient. Sometimes the consultant will take a nurse, student or house staff member, or clinical ethics trainee along for teaching purposes or as part of the consultation service.

Because the consultant most often will have spoken with the primary nurse before going to see the patient, the consultant will know when the patient is scheduled for an examination or procedure in another part of the hospital and when the patient (and the patient's significant others) will be available. Schedules vary from hospital to hospital and family to family, but it is usually best to see the patient late in the day, between 4 and 8 P.M., because this is often a time when family members can be present. The consultant should also determine from experience when physicians and the nursing staff are most available. At some time during the case, if possible, the consultant should attempt to see the patient, family members, and friends important to the case together. This allows each participant to hear the viewpoints of others and is an efficient use of time.

Table 1–2 lists ten reasons for a consultant to see a patient. The consultant should personally see the patient to gather data, because this method seems to improve the process and outcome of consultation. Seeing the patient is caring, expected, and appropriate. Seeing the patient permits focused data gathering, is convenient for the parties involved, and enables the formation of a therapeutic relationship. Seeing the patient avoids secrecy, promotes accountability, permits role modeling and teaching, provides effective case

Table 1–2   *Ten Reasons to See a Patient*

1. To gather data firsthand
2. To demonstrate caring
3. To meet clinical expectations
4. To provide convenient service
5. To form therapeutic relationships
6. To avoid secrecy
7. To promote accountability
8. To permit role modeling and teaching
9. To provide case management
10. To avoid paternalism

management, and helps to avoid paternalism by encouraging the patient's personal participation in care.

This emphasis on seeing the patient may seem dogmatic to some, but it is a natural element of the clinical approach to ethics consultation. Rather than a burdensome task, it should be energizing and engaging.

Are there any exceptions to this rule? As noted earlier in this chapter, the consultant may occasionally provide informal or curb-side information without seeing the patient. When conflicts arise between care team members (for example, whether to inform a patient about an iatrogenic error), the first step is to clarify the requester's need. Is information needed about institutional risk management or medical care? If only legal information, rather than a clinical ethical analysis, is required, it seems unnecessary to see the patient. Similarly, if the requester wants only an educational primer on truth telling and moral obligations, then a "teachable moment" in a conference room or office may suffice.

The consultant should try to see the patient alone first, which sometimes means asking family members to wait in a visitors' lounge or outside the room. Family members usually respect this request and seem to understand that the consultant may have personal matters to discuss with the patient. Even if the patient cannot discuss these or other matters, the privacy of the consultant–patient relation-ship is important and has not been emphasized enough in the ethics literature. The consultant begins by greeting the patient, introducing himself or herself, and stating the reason for the visit. At this stage in many cases, it is hard to know what will be important, so the consultant can simply observe the patient's environment (for example, lighting, books, pictures, cards, gifts, call light position, bedrails).

It is helpful to the patient and the consultant to have the attending physician inform the patient that the consultant is coming by: the patient then expects the consultant's visit, and the consultant already has familiar ground on which to stand. If the patient is physically restrained, the restraints should be untied for comfort, unless there is an obvious reason not to do so, such as imminent danger either to the patient or the consultant. The consultant can determine if the patient wants or needs something (for example, a bed adjustment, a drink of water, or a bedpan placed). The consult-ant can help the patient in these ways or find a nurse to do so. If critically ill or intubated, the patient may want to communicate by writing on a clipboard or pointing or looking at a word board. The consultant should find and provide these tools, assure the patient's comfort, and begin to listen to the patient.

Beginning the Conversation

The consultant might begin by asking whether the patient knows the reason for the consultant's visit; if not, the consultant explains the rationale for the consultation. Alternatively, the consultant may begin by discovering the patient's understanding of his or her medical problems. The consultant should already have an initial understanding of the patient's problems, gleaned from the previsit assessment and review of the medical records. Often, the consultant will find that the ethical problem is linked indirectly to the patient's medical condition. The patient who says, "I had a stroke at home and fell. When can I go home?" shows the consultant that he or she has already formulated a treatment goal.

A patient's consent to the consultation should be a part of this initial conversation; while it is rare for a patient to refuse an ethics consultation, such a refusal should be honored. If a patient refuses a consultation or if a patient's family refuses to allow the consultant to see the patient, the consultant will convey this information to the requesting physician and make a brief note to this effect in the chart. In the vast majority of cases, however, the consultation is accepted by both patient and family as individuals who care and are trying to help the patient.

The consultant makes it clear that he or she is there to help the patient. The consultant tells the patient that he or she has been asked by the attending physician to discuss several difficult and personal issues. Here is one way to open a discussion of advance directives for a patient with a stroke who has decision-making capacity but is reluctant to discuss life-sustaining treatment with the doctor or family: "Sometimes patients who have had strokes become too sick to make decisions for themselves. Would you like to talk now about how we should make decisions about breathing machines and other medical care if you become too sick to make decisions for yourself?"

After opening the conversation and then listening, the consultant can ask about the patient's goals of treatment. By asking questions along the line of the primary attending physician's request, the consultant will learn about the patient's understanding of his or her medical problems and personal situation. Sometimes, the patient seems to "solve" the ethical problem by making it clear what is wanted. If the patient's wishes are unrealistic or seem unattainable, the consultant can say so, but in a nonadversarial, nonjudgmental way, giving the patient room to think and respond. This is not as hard as it sounds, but it does require some practice. Providing information to patients, asking what they mean by a good "quality of life," reassuring them, and encouraging them to pursue their goals are central tasks of consultation.

The consultant should take advantage of patients' periods of lucidity or availability to obtain as much information then, including reasons for decisions. In the setting of waxing and waning decision-making capacity, it is especially important to call others (family members, nurses, and physicians) back in the room for conversations with such patients, because questions often arise later about the validity of such patients' statements. Comparing impressions and notes with others present at the time may be extremely helpful. In the end, facilitating communication with some patients requires good timing and good luck.

Examining the Patient

The requirement to examine patients may seem to limit the field of ethics consultation to those trained in medicine or nursing. This is not the intention, however. Consultants who do not have physical examination skills cannot be reasonably expected to acquire them. Ethics consultants who have not been trained to examine patients should make certain that the patient has been appropriately examined by others. These consultants may want to consult on a consultation service that can team them with another consultant who does have those skills.

While some may not see the need for examining a patient whose problem is ethical rather than physical, examining the patient can be important for the same reasons as seeing the patient. An examination can provide new, useful information about the patient's problems and allow the consultant to discover information that could change the case. For example, a question about whether life support should be discontinued is clarified when it is noted that the patient's midline abdominal incision has not healed after two months and that the wound is wide open; one does not need to be a surgeon or internist to make this observation. Or, a rocky hard liver in an elderly patient with a history of constipation and anemia suggests the possibility of the metastatic spread of colon cancer, which if true may greatly influence the patient's diagnosis, treatment and goals.

Table 1–3 lists the areas that should be checked in an examination. The consultant should examine the central organ system in question—heart and lungs in patients with congestive heart failure; neurologic and mental status in cognitively and psychiatrically impaired patients; pharyngeal, cervical, and abdominal areas in patients with dysphagia or recurrent aspiration. The consultant may pay special attention to the number and identity of the patient's lines, catheters, tubes, and drains. These details offer a crude index of illness severity and the current aggressiveness of medical intervention. Finally, the consultant can check for pressure sores, the complications of mechanical restraints, and the presence of ecchymoses, especially in elderly, immobile patients.

When patients cannot converse because they are neurologically, psychiatrically, or physically impaired, the consultant can still attempt to speak with them. Attempting to talk with such patients is regarded as usual practice by nursing and medical personnel, and is

Table 1–3   *The Ethics Consultant's Examination*

- **Mental status**
- **Central nervous system**
- **Major organ systems**
- **Lines, catheters, tubes, and drains**
- **Presence and effects of mechanical restraints**
- **Pressure sores and ecchymoses**

seen as humanistic and caring by family members and others. Regardless of whether the patient can understand, it is considerate to identify oneself, to give the reason for the visit, to name others with whom the consultant has been speaking, to inform the patient which organ system is about to be examined and why, and to tell the patient when the exam is over.

The consultant can also learn the key features of specialized exams from specialists. For example, the consultant can accompany a neurologist during the examination of a patient with possible persistent vegetative state. The consultant will find it helpful to carefully review the medical records for examination results.

Ethics consultants who have general examination skills will also want the assessment and advice of experts in some cases. As noted, certain elements of the exam are particularly important in ethics cases, and if the consultant is not comfortable doing these parts of the exam, he or she should make sure that they have been performed or that they will be performed. For example, when performing a consultation on a young infant with a neurological problem, the consultant should make certain that a pediatric neurologist has seen the patient. Some argue that family physicians make ideal consultants, because they can examine all patients of all ages; however, this argument ignores the reality that specialization in medicine often precludes the possibility of any one examiner knowing how to do all exams well. The insistence on a good examination is meant as a part of good clinical care.

CALLING FAMILY MEETINGS

Family meetings with and without the patient are often helpful in understanding the patient's place and role in the family. Family meetings should be conducted in an open, nonthreatening, informative way, with clearly stated goals and a time limitation set at the beginning. Whenever possible, the attending physician should lead the meeting, since he or she is primarily responsible for the patient's care. When the physician is poorly equipped or asks the consultant to lead the meeting, the consultant should step into this role, attempting to model proper patient-centered and family-centered interviewing techniques. Family meeting caveats include the following:

- Invite key players only
- Limit the size of meeting
- Bring an attorney if the family's attorney attends
- Encourage an open atmosphere
- Focus on areas of agreement and future goals

Family meetings are also helpful to the health care team. They may bring together physicians, nurses, and social workers who may have never discussed the patient's case together and who may want to discuss findings, impressions, and subtleties not found in the medical record.

When the patient has decision-making capacity, family meetings should focus on what the patient says. When there is disagreement among family members about the authenticity of the patient's wishes or about the course of treatment to pursue, the consultant can assist by interviewing the patient and family separately and then together, usually in the patient's room. This method is helpful if the patient wishes to keep a secret from the family, if the patient has different goals and objectives than the family, or if the patient tends to change his or her mind in the presence of strong or persuasive family members. The consultant's role is to enable the patient to articulate his or her interests and, when possible, achieve his or her stated goals.

The issue is different, however, when the patient has decision-making capacity and family members disagree, for example, about when or how to tell the patient the diagnosis or likely prognosis. Family meetings then serve to redirect the discussion toward the patient's own value system and circumstances. The consultant can reinforce the usual primacy of the patient's wishes, take the patient's side, and attempt to promote a discussion between patient and family.

When patients are unable to make decisions themselves, family members can inquire about and receive information about the patient's case, enabling them to act as medically informed surrogate decision makers. The consultant can facilitate these meetings by making family members comfortable and stating the goals of the meeting, the timetable, and other limitations. Sometimes, a second or third meeting is needed to clarify uncertain or pending medical or personal values, to include a just-arrived family member or friend, or to give the family time together. By respecting the relationship between the primary attending physician and family members and by defusing hostility (by being factual and clear, guiding feuding key players to the same side of the table, and attempting to depersonalize disagreements), the consultant can, with luck and skill, improve the dynamics of family meetings.

Family members are usually important, powerful, and articulate patient advocates, especially when the patient is incompetent, elderly, or disabled. It cannot be said often enough, however, that a patient and his family frequently have different agendas, goals, interests, and objectives. So first, the consultant scrutinizes the patient's history of clinical choices and possibilities. Second, the consultant analyzes whether the patient's wishes and choices and those of the family are compatible.

Some consultants strive to bring together all members of the family, health care team, and interested parties to discuss the issues, in hope that any tension can be abated by group discussion. Many consultants, however, try to avoid large family meetings. Large family meetings may feel like jury trials, especially to patients and their families, and may serve to exacerbate existing tension and adversity. These meetings are often unwieldy, poorly focused, unproductive, and less open and democratic than they might appear. Some members of the family with minority views on the issues at hand may be unable to speak freely in these forums. Sometimes, however, these large meetings have already been arranged by another member of the health care team and cannot be avoided.

Occasionally, patients' or families' attorneys attend family meetings, and although such attorneys are often well intentioned, they are often not well informed about health care matters unless they happen to specialize in health law. When attorneys attend family meetings, the consultant usually asks the hospital attorney to attend too. The hospital attorney knows health law, has the interests of the hospital and the consultant in mind, and can support the health professionals involved. Family meetings with attorneys present tend to be adversarial. When the consultant participates in these meetings, attempts should be made to conduct them with clinically-centered, non-legalistic goals in mind. Such goals include, for example, securing permission for a transfusion in a light-headed, anemic patient or diminishing a niece's feeling of fault that she delayed too long before calling an ambulance for her now-critically-ill aunt who had a large stroke.

Often, family meetings are called to clarify areas of disagreement or, even more specifically, to attempt to persuade family members of something to which they should agree. The key to finding areas of agreement is to ask family members to focus on what the adult patient would want or, for a pediatric patient, what is in the child's best interest. Many family members will try hard to put aside their own agendas and can sometimes differentiate their own desires from those of the patient.

Some families, however, may not be able to think of the patient's own wishes aside from their own, especially parents of young children or the adult children of elderly patients. It is important in these cases to get a sense of the patient's values and to relieve the family of the burden of the decision by attempting to focus on the patient's preferences and possibilities. Similarly, some patients consider themselves to be more a member of their family than a distinct individual. These patients will not easily (and should not be forced to) separate their own desires from their family's. When family unity is the patient's and family's most important value, separation is inappropriate. Lifting the burden of decision-making requires considering the patient as a family member more than as an individual. These patients and families may make decisions as a unit. The consultant's role is to understand and accept these values, respect them, and integrate them into an ethical analysis.

PREPARING AN ETHICAL ANALYSIS

In case consultation, no single ethical principle suffices. Cases vary too much to make such generalizations. The consultant usually allows the details of the case to frame the issues; the consultation process allows the patient, family, and caretakers to identify the important factors and values at stake. This modern medical casuistry — solving cases by considering the clinical circumstances that surround and affect the cases, instead of by applying a set of rules or principles to them — characterizes the ethical analysis that the consultant performs. This method of analysis uses the internal elements of the case rather than external elements, such as codes or theory (see Table 1–4). Cases are grouped together based on how they appear overall.

Likewise, while some ethics consultants advocate structured, formal frameworks for clinical decision-making, most consultants actually apply such constructs gently and with great caution. Intuition, metaphor, common sense, religious tradition, hospital policy, or state law could be the crucial factor in a particular consultation. Ethics consultants must be flexible and view a case depending on the clinical details given and discovered. The ethics consultant's axiom might be something like: "I will attempt to understand all the relevant particular elements of a case, clarify treatment goals, and propose ethically acceptable actions." Consultants should be persistent in their pursuit of this goal. When they fail, it is often not so much in the analysis of an issue, but in the paucity of details and data gathered. Thus, the importance of a careful search for information has been emphasized throughout this book.

The consultant can almost always assess the following key items for each patient:

- The patient's goals and objectives
- Options for treatment plans
- The patient's decision-making capacity
- Whether a DNR (do not resuscitate) order is appropriate
- The presence of a written advance directive
- Any conflict with applicable health care law

Table 1–4   Steps in Case Analysis

- Articulate patient's goals and objectives
- Search for advance directives or proxies
- Describe treatment options
- Construct decision-making framework
- Discuss financial elements
- Delineate applicable principles, if any
- Propose a range of acceptable options

- The financial elements and constraints of the case
- Whether the patient needs a proxy decision maker, and, if so, who that might be and whether that person is reliable and well intentioned.

Most analyses are a mix of clinical, ethical, and legal factors. Examples of case assessments are presented in the Appendix.

Ethical analysis should focus on outlining several courses of action and attempting to discern which courses of action are ethically desirable, permissible, or appropriate. The information gathered from the patient, primary attending physician, records, nurses, and family members usually provide the deciding elements of this analysis.

In many cases, critical information is missing and must be gathered, analyzed, and integrated before an assessment can be made. Sources may be unavailable (for example, the patient's sister, a hospital attorney, or a national expert on liver transplantation), or tests may be pending (for example, a second ELISA determination for HIV or a pathology report). While waiting for missing information, or when the case is especially challenging or new, the consultant often does extra reading to gather additional information that may be useful. Sometimes, the consultant searches for new medical and ethical data about a problem (for example, the efficacy and safety of mechanical restraints; the reversibility of pressure sores; the validity of proxy decision-making about CPR, quality of life, or mechanical ventilation; or the professional conflicts in the treatment of medical students, VIPs, or a physician's own family members). The consultant may reread classic articles (for example, to elucidate a difficult decision about decision-making capacity) or sections of textbooks or sourcebooks (such as *Clinical Ethics, Ethics and the Regulation of Clinical Research,* or *The President's Commission* series). The consultant may also discuss the case with a clinical ethicist colleague.

In cases where the consultant has all the particular patient-centered information but lacks specific data about the natural history of a disease, innovative articles, papers, and policies may help inform the consultant. The consultant's job is to answer the primary physician's question; to identify, clarify, and analyze the ethical issues in the case; and to show the primary physician the process of reaching an assessment and recommended plan.

Of course, there are cases with an abundance of information that are still difficult to resolve. Some of these cases can be resolved in time, while the consultant follows along. In other cases, the ethical dilemma is resolved in the hospital, but time helps outside the hospital. In rare cases, more time and more and better analysis do not help, and there is no resolution.

It is as difficult to explain how to do an ethical analysis in particular cases as it is to describe the inner workings of a close doctor–patient relationship. The truth is that such analysis is often learned by watching other consultants, by doing a number of cases and seeing how things work out, and by obtaining feedback from patients, attending physicians, and colleagues.

The Clinical Scope of Consultation and Analysis

The scope of most consultations is limited to particular clinical issues. The clinicians caring for the patient are concerned about a resolution to the ethical dilemma at hand. Policy-oriented discussions of health care are interesting, but of more immediate concern, for example, is how to get a critically ill patient an intensive care unit bed in a full hospital or how to get a patient the liver transplant he or she needs to survive.

When the consultant is asked whether it is appropriate to consider a patient for liver transplantation, he or she should ask: What are the likely medical risks and benefits of transplantation for this particular patient with hepatic failure? What is the patient's personal situation? What is the availability of donor livers? These patient-centered questions and facts are aligned with, but distinct from, the policy-centered questions of whether the recipient selection process should incorporate psychosocial criteria or whether all patients "deserve" transplants. Of course, the ethicist is interested in these questions, but what is important to the patient and requesting physician should take precedence.

In another example, the ethics consultant is often asked to make an assessment of decision-making capacity. Currently, no validated, standardized bedside tools exist for evaluating decision-making capacity. Formal mental status examination and neuropsychological testing are usually not decisive, although a mental status exam may rule out gross psychosis. A patient's decision-making capacity is as specific as the decision to be made. Ascertaining whether a patient has the capacity to refuse a specific treatment involves determining if he or she understands the nature of the disease, the treatment(s) being offered, the likely consequences of refusing the treatment(s), and any alternatives to treatment(s). The patient should also be able to integrate information into his or her own value system, articulate a cogent reason for the refusal, and actually have the ability to choose.

The consultant can contrast the individuality of this assessment with the general direction given by health care law or psychiatric and psychologic evaluation instruments. According to public policy and common law, patients are competent until proven incompetent in court. It is the consultant's bedside particularity and personal focus that place an assessment of decision-making capacity within the scope of clinical ethics.

TALKING WITH THE REQUESTING PHYSICIAN

The consultant often speaks with the attending physician again before writing a report and dictating the consultation. Even when the case seems to end in a big family meeting with the attending physician present, the consultant should have a conversation with the attending.

After the consultant has formulated an analysis, and sometimes sketched recommendations on paper, he or she can call the primary attending physician to report personally findings and recommendations. This conversation is an opportunity to demonstrate to a colleague the mechanism of analysis in the case, and to show which personal and medical details contribute most. Geriatric and general medicine consultation services report that compliance with their recommendations is facilitated by personal contact.[1,2] This is likely to prove true for ethics consultation as well.

During the conversation, a time frame for accomplishing suggestions can be laid out, and often in more detail than in a written note. This conversation is expected and often may be collegial and reassuring, especially when the case is complex. The consultant will discover that requesting physicians almost always look forward to such a discussion and are appreciative of any efforts that help them handle the case and others like it. The consultant can clarify for the attending when he or she will see the patient again.

This postconsultation conversation is also important because it sets the stage for the necessary follow-up process. For example, speaking with the requesting physician is necessary before writing a report; if the recommendations included reversing a treatment plan or disagreeing with others, the consultant would want to be sure that the primary physician understood these suggestions before they were entered as part of a legal document.

WRITING A REPORT

After the consultant–physician conversation, the consultant can write a full report for the medical record. Writing a report is important for the following reasons:

1. Colleagues expect it.
2. Other members of the health care team with whom the consultant has not been able to speak may be curious about the consultant's analysis or recommendations.
3. The consultant collects his or her thoughts in recording the consultation, sometimes working out what he or she thinks about a case while writing.
4. The reports become part of the patient's legal medical record and document the consultant's work — the gathered and reviewed data, including who was interviewed and when, what they had to say, and who was not interviewed and why.

In a sense, reports evidence legitimacy and offer a clear, familiar path for the reader to follow, showing the basis for the consultant's suggestions.

When the ethics consultant begins to record the consultation, he or she may first write a progress note entitled "Clinical Ethics Consultation." This note reports the question that the consultant has been asked to address, as well as who requested the consultation. The consultant records the attending's (previously voiced) approval of the request for consultation. The ethics consultant records whether he or she has seen and examined the patient and the content of any relevant patient or family interviews. If the consultant needs to gather more medical data, conduct a family meeting, or speak with an outside expert before giving a formal opinion, he or she can list these as planned actions and make only a tentative, general assessment of the patient's medical and personal situation, noting that recommendations and references will follow. If the consultant does not need to gather more data, he or she can write an assessment of the ethical dilemmas at hand, trying to address the attending physician's question. The consultant should enumerate recommendations, list references, and sign the document.

In addition to the progress note just described, the general ethics consultation format in Table 1–5 may be used to record a full consultation. Such a format can be useful for both the requesting physician's and the ethics consultant's records.

Table 1–5   *Format for Formal Consultation Report*

1. Patient name, medical record number, location, room number, date of consultation, and date of admission
2. Quoted question asked; requester identified
3. History of present illness
4. Hospital course, with problem list
5. Other consultations, if relevant
6. Medications
7. Social, personal, and familial history
8. Pertinent physical examination
9. Pertinent laboratory data
10. Assessment
11. Discussion
12. Recommendations
13. References
14. Copies to others

Writing Recommendations

Many consultants attempt to write no more than four recommendations, listed in decreasing order of importance. Reviews of the medical consultation literature have shown four recommendations to be the most to which requesting physicians pay attention.[2] These recommendations are written in the progress note and, when possible, dictated verbatim in the full consultation report for consistency. If the ethics consultant has additional recommendations to make the next day, they are again written in the progress notes. If there are nuances in the recommendations, they should be discussed personally with the requesting physician.

Recommendations are written as suggestions and usually prefaced with "Attempt to . . . ," or "Suggest," both for the sake of the requesting physician (in case he or she is unable or prefers not to accomplish these tasks) and for others (to leave other options open, as well as to avoid potential legal conflict). If the consultant offers recommendations that run counter to the present course and knows that the physician cannot or will not agree, the consultant should still write them as suggestions and list references to support this suggested plan of action.

Unexpected written recommendations may cause trouble. For example, pedantic and impractical recommendations will usually be ignored. Discussing the general importance of durable powers of attorney for health care in a case where the existing DPA manifests clear conflicts of interest is not helpful. The consultant should save the lecture for the classroom. Strident and immediately directive recommendations may have to be rebutted by the attending physician; they also pose potential legal problems for all, perhaps without helping the patient. The consultant should discuss written recommendations before writing them.

On the other hand, if the consultant merely provides advice that is known to be popular, without adequate ethical justification, the consultation process becomes reassurance rather than constructive analysis. Consultants earn clinical respect when they are honest and willing to grapple with a case even when it is uncomfortable and their recommendations are unpopular. Consultants are rarely, if ever, asked to sacrifice their job over a case. Even a careful ethics consultant, however, can make powerful colleagues angry on occasion if the advice offered is not the advice desired. This is part of the risk of the job.

Providing References

The consultant can use reference articles in several ways: to demonstrate why a particular assessment and recommendation was made in the case; to teach trainees who are learning to do consultations; to provide the health care team with a practical, published framework for considering the problem; to educate attendings, house staff, and students who want a published framework for considering cases; and to gain a sense from the literature available of how to address the problem at hand.

Journal article references are useful in some cases, but they can also be problematic. Articles in philosophy journals, law journals, and many subspecialty medical journals are often too complex to be helpful, and go unread. "Throwaway" medical journal articles sometimes oversimplify solutions, providing rote remedies to ethical problems. Nevertheless, careful searching can reveal useful references, such as key medical ethics textbooks and papers written in peer-reviewed medical journals. In academia, or when a case is especially difficult, controversial, or clinically complex, the consultant will probably do best to list and supply references from high-impact medical journals.

When the consultant places articles in the reference list, they should be specific, to the point, and directly concern the case problems. Only occasionally is it necessary to use general references on informed consent, for example, or the withdrawal of life-sustaining treatment. Medically specific literature may also be useful; for example, the consultant may provide articles about postpartum psychosis to a health care team treating a pregnant manic-depressive patient, or about prognosis in penetrating head injury for a team service treating a patient with a gunshot wound to the head.

EFFECTING ETHICAL OUTCOMES

Can ethics consultation improve the ethical outcome of cases? This is a critical question, because a central purpose of ethics consultation is to help effect an ethical outcome.

An ethical outcome is commensurate with the patient's good, given the medical facts and personal circumstances. An ethical outcome is also an ideal, one that requires the doctor and patient to work together toward a mutually agreed upon goal. The doctor–patient accommodation shows respect to patients and their families, with their (sometimes differing) interests, needs, and objectives; shows compassion for patients, at all times, even to the point of altruism; and demonstrates decency, honesty, and fairness. In striving for an ethical outcome, the ethics consultant attempts to encourage this doctor–patient accommodation and works to achieve an out-come that Kass calls the "just right thing to do" in a given clinical situation.[3]

One way to evaluate the outcome of ethics consultation is to perform empiric studies (see Table 1–6). In one study, an ethics consultation service at a university medical center saw 51 patients from July 1986 through June 1987.[4] Seventeen of the 51 patients (33 percent) were in the ICU, and 19 patients (37 percent) were fully oriented at the time of consultation; overall, 61 percent survived to leave the hospital. Assistance with more than one issue was sought in 39 cases (76 percent). The requesting physician sought assistance with withholding or withdrawing life-sustaining treatment in 49

Table 1–6   *Two Empiric Studies of Ethics Consultation: University/Community Hospitals*

Patients in the ICU (33%–69%)
Patients fully oriented (37%)
Patients survived to leave hospital (61%)
Assistance with more than one issue (76%)
Withholding/withdrawing issues (49%–59%)
Resolving disagreements (40%)
Resuscitation issues (37%)
Legal issues (31%)
Determining decision-making capacity (29%)
Requesting physician states consult "very important" (71%)
Requesting physician would request a consult in the future (95%)

percent of the cases, with resuscitation issues in 37 percent of the cases, and with legal issues in 31 percent of the cases.

At a community teaching hospital, 104 patients were seen consecutively from January 1988 through December 1989.[5] Of the 51 patients (49 percent) who had decision-making capacity at the time of consultation, 31 (62 percent) thought their cases raised ethical issues. Most often, the requesting physician sought help with deciding to forego life-sustaining treatment (59 percent of the cases), resolving disagreements with family or others (40 percent), and determining patient competence (29 percent).

Another way to assess the outcome of ethics consultation is to ask requesters about their experience with the consultation. In both studies, more than 95 percent of the physicians stated that they would request another ethics consultation in the future. In 36 of the cases (71 percent) at the university medical center, the requesting physician stated that the consult was "very important" in patient management, in the clarification of ethical issues, or in the teaching of medical ethics.[4] In 86 percent of the cases[5] at the community teaching hospital, the requesting physician stated that the consult was "very helpful" or "helpful" in one or more aspects of patient care or in one or more aspects of physician education.

Whether physicians who request ethics consultations are more interested in ethical issues, have more complex patients, or are more sophisticated (or more naive) about ethical issues than physicians who do not request consultations is unknown. Only preliminary data are available about the consultation's effect on requesters. In the community hospital study, 19 requesting physicians (23 percent) reported that they had some "background in ethics, bioethics or clinical ethics."[6] Sixty-six respondents (81 percent) reported discussing the ethical issues in the case with other physicians; 31 discussed them with the patient; 22 discussed them with their spouse; 11 discussed them with the patient's family; 2 discussed them with clergy; and 1 discussed them with a lawyer. Sixty-four physician respondents (77 percent) reported discussions with more than one person.

Outcomes assessment is the touchstone of quality improvement. Thus, reasonable patient-centered and physician-centered outcomes could serve as quality indicators for ethics consultation (see Table 1–7). Such outcomes may include the following:

1. Patients or their surrogates perceive the consultant as someone who was personally involved in their care, who had a clinician–patient relationship with them.
2. Patients or their surrogates perceive that the consultation process sought out their goals and values, and their active participation in decision-making.
3. Patients or their surrogates perceive themselves as understanding alternatives, risks, and benefits, and are able to describe their knowledge and understanding of what has been discussed.
4. Physicians perceive the consultant as having become knowledgeable about and involved in the care of the patient, and as having been helpful or important enough to request future consultations in other cases, if needed.
5. Physicians perceive themselves as having a better understanding of the ethical issues in the case and better prepared for future cases, and are able to describe their increased knowledge and understanding.
6. Physicians perceive that their decisions were made in collaboration with patients or their surrogates, and that the consultation enhanced the decision-making process or the care of the patient.
7. Patients, families, physicians, and third parties are less likely to perceive the costs of care delivered in pursuit of shared goals as excessive.[7] (Table 1–7)

Other methods of assessing outcome are possible. These include examining any changes in the process of clinical decision making,

Table 1–7   *Potential Quality Indicators for Ethics Consultation*

- Consultant is personally involved in the case.
- The process supports patient's goals and values.
- Alternatives are described.
- The consultant is perceived as useful.
- Requesting physicians describe increased knowledge.
- Requesting physicians perceive collaboration.
- There is a reduction in futile and excessive treatment.
- There is an increase in desired and useful treatment.

evaluating patients' and families' satisfaction with the consultation, and assessing the cost-effectiveness of ethics consultation in helping patients avoid unwanted care or gain access to needed care. Most institutional ethics consultants, however, prefer physician-based outcomes (for example, the consultant's effect on case management and physician education) as well as patient-based outcomes (for example, the consultant's personal involvement in the case and role in seeking out patient goals, values, and participation in decision making).

Whether consultations can be considered successful will also depend not just on the empiric measurement of satisfaction and cost-effectiveness, but also on the value of the consultation process. What is meant by a good "process" of ethics consultation? The consultative process is formed by the various elements of information gathering, case analysis, and interpersonal communication. Discovering new clinical information, discussing concerns with the patient and family, exchanging views and elucidating values, identifying achievable goals that fit the medical details and the patient's personal situation, and recommending means of achieving these goals are all part of the process of ethics consultation.

Speaking with patients, families, and the health care team is the major activity of the process. Patients especially desire information, reassurance, encouragement, and permission, not just prescriptions and procedures. Consultation takes extra time because it must accommodate interpersonal variables that vary even more than technical or physical variables. Consultation involves a painstaking cognitive process, approaching issues of complex, multifactorial decision making often associated with complex medical and personal stories. From start to finish, a full ethics consultation performed by an experienced consultant requires an average of three to four hours to perform.

FOLLOWING UP

The consultant should attempt to see the patient again the day after the initial consultation. If the patient is critically ill and is being extubated (for example, in the ICU), it may be necessary to see him or her several times in a day.

Several reasons support close follow-up. Cases change quickly, and different ethical issues can arise literally overnight. A family member could arrive on the scene and provide information that could not be obtained previously. The patient's medical condition could change, and the results of treatments or tests (or their absence) could influence the patient's decisions or potential choices. In addition, requesting physicians appreciate having a consultant follow a patient; close follow-up shows the consultant's interest in the patient. Case follow-up enables the consultant to review and revise the assessment and recommendations, correct mistakes, sign the dictated or otherwise recorded report, and place references in the medical record.

When patients are in the hospital for long periods of time, it is not necessary to see them daily, but the consultant can keep in touch with the patient's primary physician. Knowing the medical and personal details of the patient's case, the ethics consultant can offer timely and relevant counsel. In this way, dated and superfluous hypotheses can be avoided.

CASE CLOSE

In the case of Mr. Garcia, the consultant might have imagined that the case was one of clinical futility. After all, the patient had received massive transfusion support. According to the phone conversation with the fellow, further treatment seemed futile. But at the bedside, the consultant found a subtly different story. While Mr. Garcia was in liver failure, jaundiced and encephalopathic, he was also able to nod his head appropriately to questions. When the consultant saw him, he was able to respond that he did not have any pain and that he did want treatment. Examination revealed ascites, but not tense ascites. The protime was 16, as opposed to 20, and there was some hope for hepatic recovery. An endoscopy had not revealed esophageal varices; the patient was bleeding from severe gastritis from a recent drinking bout.

In this case, the consultant recommended continued support with blood products for now, and offered to follow

continued

along. These recommendations were written in the chart. Because of the personal nature of the fact gathering and the use of a patient-oriented focus, the consultant was able to avoid the mistake of agreeing that the patient's case was futile just because it sounded hopeless over the phone. As it turned out, Mr. Garcia survived with normal neurologic function and went home.

ILLUSTRATIVE CASES

The Appendix contains a number of illustrative cases and their resolutions. The reader may gain a sense of how consultation proceeds by reading through these cases.

SUMMARY

Requests for formal ethics consultation come primarily from attending physicians for their hospitalized patients. The attending must agree to a consultation if it is someone else's idea.

After a request is received, the consultant speaks with the requesting physician and helps to define the requesting physician's goals for the consultation. Then the consultant talks with the primary nurse and the patient's friends and family members.

Before seeing the patient, the consultant scrutinizes the medical record. The record provides historical, medical, and temporal perspectives on the case.

The consultant's own notes reflect the importance of the gathered data to the patient's problems. The consultant should list the date of admission, admitting diagnosis, admitting physician, consulting physicians, medical problems and working diagnoses, current and recently discontinued medications, relevant family members with phone numbers, and relevant and pending laboratory findings, such as the HIV antibody status in an intravenous drug abuser or the peripheral white count and differential in a patient with leukemia.

After the initial discussions and review of the hospital record, the ethics consultant is ready to see the patient. The interview begins with the consultant asking if the patient knows the reason for the visit; if the patient does not know, the consultant explains the rationale for the consultation. Seeing the patient is important because the consultant can gather information firsthand, demonstrate caring, meet clinical expectations, provide convenient service, form a therapeutic relationship, avoid secrecy, promote accountability, role model and teach, provide case management, and avoid paternalism.

Examining patients is important for the same reasons as seeing the patient. Often, examining patients provides new, useful information. If the consultant is not a physician, he or she can still make sure that the patient has been properly examined by the appropriate specialist.

After seeing and examining the patient, the consultant often meets with the patient's family. Family meetings are often useful. Meetings should be direct and time-limited, and goals should be clearly stated at the beginning.

The consultant usually uses the details of the case to frame and analyze the issues. Before writing a report, the consultant talks with the attending physician. After this conversation, the consultant often writes a full report.

When the ethics consultant records the consultation in the medical record, the progress note describes the question that the consultant has been asked to address. The consultant records seeing the patient, and the content of any relevant patient or family interviews. If more medical information or another family meeting is needed, he or she can list these planned actions and make only a tentative, general assessment of the patient's medical and personal situation, noting that recommendations and references will follow.

The consultant often makes no more than four recommendations, writing them in decreasing order of importance. These recommendations are written in the progress notes, and dictated or otherwise recorded in the full consultation report for consistency.

The consultant can provide written, peer-reviewed, published references that are specific and practical to the health care team when a case is especially difficult or when the team desires them.

Attempting to effect an ethical outcome in a case is a central goal of consultation. An ethical outcome is commensurate with the patient's good as he or she helps to determine it, given the medical facts and personal circumstances. Outcome and process are linked in ethics consultation. Enhancing the doctor–patient relationship and spending enough careful, attentive time with patients are key ways of effecting good outcomes.

The process of ethics consultation involves follow-up. The consultant attempts to see patients the day after the initial consultation. Cases change quickly, and different issues can arise overnight. Patients and requesting physicians appreciate having a consultant follow the case closely. Follow-up demonstrates that the consultant is concerned about the patient.

2

Training, Skills, and Certification

Whenever possible, consultants take trainees to the bedside.

Ethics consultation, as discussed in Chapter 1, requires active investigation. Consultants interview and, when appropriate, examine the patient, speak with the patient's family, discuss the case with members of the health care team, review the hospital chart, and document recommendations in the patient's medical record. Because consultants serve individual patients, they can discover and bring together the relevant ethical aspects of a patient's history and medical condition, identify the opposing arguments or values of those involved, and restore a central ethical focus to a patient's case. Here is a case in which the consultant employs consultation skills to do just that.

> Mark Kennedy is a 22-year-old man on probation for retail theft. Last year, he graduated from an alcohol rehabilitation program. He won't go to jail so long as he doesn't drink, holds a job, and lives at home.
>
> Three months ago, Mr. Kennedy moved out of his parents' house and began drinking. Around midnight on the day of admission, he loaded three friends who are brothers (ages 11, 12, and 13) into his car and drove with the lights off into a tree. In the Emergency Department, his alcohol level was 0.25; he had a wide mediastinum and was unconscious. The 12-year-old passenger escaped with minor injuries, but the 11-year-old died, and the 13-year-old was in a coma.
>
> The on-call surgeon took Mr. Kennedy to the operating suite, repaired an aortic arch tear, and resected the left upper lobe of his lung. Mr. Kennedy slowly recovered and in three months he was able to speak and to walk despite gangrene of six toes.
>
> Mr. Kennedy remembered nothing about the accident. His probation officer recommended sending him to jail. The rehabilitation unit physician wondered: What are my ethical obligations to ensure that Mr. Kennedy receives good

outpatient care, given his need for further cognitive rehab? Is he competent to go to jail? How do I tell him what he has done? Given his social history, is more money really well spent?

The consultant examined Mr. Kennedy, noting his cognitive deficits, multiple scars, and dry gangrene. The consultant spoke with Mr. Kennedy and, during the conversation, noted that Mr. Kennedy was unable to put on his socks by himself. The consultant spoke with Mr. Kennedy's mother, who had told him about his accident when he was home once on weekend pass. The patient's first reaction was to cry, but later he said, "Well, it was the car's fault. The car killed him."

The consultant interviewed the patient's social worker and asked the social worker to find out more about the health facilities available in jail. The consultant also asked hospital counsel about the process of arrest, arraignment, charges, and bail. Finally, the consultant reviewed the literature concerning physicians' obligations to assess and treat mentally ill patients so that they may stand trial.

The individual consultant approach described in this case allows for active bedside evaluation, and is the subject of this book. The following discussion will highlight the merits of several other ethics consultation approaches currently in use, and will examine the issues of training, skills, and certification.

APPROACHES TO ETHICS CONSULTATION

Some advocate that patients and families should choose the type of approach used by the consultant. Despite favorable experience with the individual consultant and consultation service/team, the approaches used in various settings may differ based on the strength of ethics committees and of committee chairs, the nature of the ethics program at the institution, and the services required by patients. This pluralism of consultation seems wise and appropriate. But patients usually expect a personal approach to care. Empiric studies show a high degree of requesting physician satisfaction with consultation services.[1,2] These initial observations suggest that different clinical consultation services deserve special exploration and development.

Consultation Service

Ethics consultations can be performed by an individual consultant on a consultation service.[3,4] The advantages of this approach include the ease of its clinical "fit," its emphasis on personal service, and its ready acceptance by patients and professionals. Practitioners see the patient promptly and provide follow-up as needed. Other consultation services, such as those of medical and surgical subspecialties, may employ a similar, hands-on approach.

Consultation services usually include a number of practitioners sharing responsibilities. Ethics consultants and consultation services are more likely to be available in large teaching institutions or medical schools than in other settings. The disadvantages of this approach include a lack of trained practitioners, concerns about accountability, and problems with reimbursement.

Ethics Committee Subcommittee

A consulting subcommittee of the institutional ethics committee can bring complementary viewpoints to the management of particular cases.[5,6] Chapter 4 provides more information about consulting subcommittees. Occasionally, subcommittees are led by trained ethics consultants; members can save the consultant time and the consultant can help to train subcommittee members. Ordinarily, however, the subcommittee attempts to pool ethics expertise when no individual member is trained and available to perform consultation. The subcommittee usually reports to the ethics committee before or after consulting.

This approach is less personal and slower than a consultation service. While the subcommittee can provide administrative accountability, it diffuses responsibility for patient care. In addition, some members of the subcommittee may lack clinical credibility and ethics training. This approach has some acceptance in health care institutions that do not have a trained ethics consultant on staff.

Ethics Committee

Ethics committees can perform ethics consultations as an entire group.[7,8] While these committees can act as sounding boards, and bring multidisciplinary perspectives to cases, they are usually not trained in consultation. While most hospitals in the country have committees, a consensus is emerging that these committees work best in a policy-making and educational role rather than in a bedside consultation role.

Committees can seem impersonal and remote to patients and families. When patients and families face the entire committee, they may perceive it as a quasi-judicial body. As administrative bodies, they can be very slow in acting, compared with the individual consultant or even the ethics committee subcommittee. While the committee was initially favored as the ideal consultation approach by many ethicists, most now believe that other approaches to consultation offer better service to patients and staff.

Choosing an Approach

Regardless of the model chosen, the clinical approach to ethics consultation seems the most patient centered and humanistic. The clinical approach can be incorporated into the ethics subcommittee and committee if a member of the committee functions as an ethics consultant. Detailed discussions of the advantages and disadvantages of each approach are beyond the scope of this book.

LEGITIMACY AND ACCOUNTABILITY

The authority for ethics consultation may arise from several sources. The primary moral justification for ethics consultation derives from the mandate to protect the patient and foster shared decision making in the clinical setting. Originating from the President's Commission's recommendations for ethical practice more than a decade ago, this mandate helps to create a place for ethics consultants in health care settings. The American College of Physicians and the American Medical Association recognize that protecting and enhancing shared doctor–patient decision-making is an ethical responsibility. The courts and presidential commissions have recommended that clinicians seek appropriate assistance in making ethical decisions.

In ideal practice, physicians share health care decisions with well-informed, decisionally capable patients who understand their diagnoses, prognoses, and the various alternatives of proposed treatment and of nontreatment. In actual practice, and when an ethical problem arises that neither the patient nor the physician can solve, ethics consultation can assure that issues are clarified so that shared decision-making can occur.

Mutual participation in decision-making represents a shift in focus for doctors and patients. Traditionally, there has been little accommodation of patients' values by physicians. Shared decision-making occurs when the doctor and patient integrate the patient's values and goals and the doctor's knowledge of the clinical condition. The patient's perception of his or her clinical condition and the doctor's personal value system also influence a decision. The consultant knows that fostering and endorsing such decision-making is an ideal that requires patience, effort, time, and skill.

The primary clinical justification for ethics consultation originates in the doctor–patient relationship. Either the doctor or the patient may need assistance. Requests for this type of assistance are relatively new. Such requests arise from clinical needs — the doctor's need for analysis and advice in individual patient cases, the patient's need for an advocate, and the institution's need for counsel in patient-related policy issues. While many new areas of endeavor may appear to lack legitimacy, these broad-based health care needs seem to suggest a strong "legitimacy" for ethics consultation.

Ethics consultants are primarily accountable to individual patients and physicians, but consultants can also be accountable to institutional bodies, professional associations, and government agencies. One of us (J.L.) works primarily as a clinical practitioner within a consultation service. He must be licensed by the state to practice medicine, and he is accountable to his colleagues in peer-review, to the medical staff for ethics consultation privileges, and to institutional sponsors of the service. He presents completed cases at a weekly case conference for discussion with colleagues from chaplaincy, law, social services, medicine and nursing. His consultations may draw on other individual experts from outside the consultation service (for example, specialty nurses and health care attorneys). The other (D.S.) is accountable to his ethics committee. Occasionally, he involves the entire ethics committee, particularly to allow the committee to participate in the discussion of cases that present policy issues. His ethics committee is sponsored and legitimized by the medical staff and appointed by the medical staff president.

Both forms of consultation require similar skills on the part of the consultant, and both provide the consultant with legitimacy, accountability, and backup. Legitimacy and accountability permit the consultant to work effectively within boundaries.

THE GROWTH AND DEVELOPMENT OF ETHICS CONSULTATION

When ethics consultants first became available to their colleagues in the 1970s, the consultants began to question whether their work constituted a distinct professional activity. Many consultative fields in medicine (for example, rheumatology, cardiology, psychiatry, and geriatrics) began in a similar way, as practitioners developed a new knowledge base and found a growing demand for their specialized skills.

The discipline of clinical ethics has slowly gained recognition in the academic, practice, and scientific communities. Ethics publications in peer-reviewed medical journals are now considered legitimate contributions when academic physicians are evaluated for promotion. The number of practitioners in clinical ethics has grown dramatically since the 1970s. In 1985, only 51 consultants attended a NIH/UCSF exploratory meeting; currently, there are over 2,000 ethics consultants.

Modern American medical ethics began with the writings of several physician–leaders in the early twentieth century. Cabot described the physician's ethical obligations to tell the truth to patients. Peabody wrote, "One of the essential qualities of the clinician is interest in humanity, for the secret of the care of the patient is in caring for the patient." Henderson described the doctor-patient relationship as a social system, showing how doctor and patient teamwork could enhance clinical outcomes.

Tentative exploration of hospital ethics consultation began in the late 1960s and early 1970s at Penn State, Columbia P and S, and the New Jersey College of Medicine. In the late 1970s, Fletcher at the National Institutes of Health (NIH) Clinical Center gained experience with clinical ethical dilemmas in a research hospital, assisting investigators and patients with problems of informed consent and confidentiality. In 1978 and 1979, Siegler and Pellegrino published a series of papers that outlined a role for clinical ethics as a special field of expertise in medicine. In 1980, Jonsen asked, "Can an ethicist be a consultant?" Jonsen's paper was the first to discuss the process of ethics consultation, and the first to discuss the merits and pitfalls of consultation.

In 1982, the handbook *Clinical Ethics* was published. Written by a philosopher, an internist, and an attorney, and designed to fit into an intern's pocket, the book provided short, to-the-point analyses and outlined a clinician-friendly, four-point method for analyzing ethical problems. In 1985, the NIH/UCSF joint conference on ethics consultation was held, to which 51 invited consultants and 20 invited observers came. After this meeting, a Society for Bioethics Consultation (SBC) was organized to attempt to draw in those already engaged in consultation.

Ethics consultation is developing and growing (see Table 2–1). In 1987, the first empiric study of ethics consultation in the peer-reviewed medical literature was published, describing 27 cases in which an ethicist had been asked for assistance and detailing the consultant's method for organizing replies to such requests. In 1988, Pellegrino noted that with the practice of clinical ethics came a wonderful opportunity to study human values, ethical assumptions, and patient preferences. In 1990, the first issue of a journal devoted to clinical ethics was published. Also in 1990, a national symposium on research methods in clinical ethics was held at the annual meeting of the Society for General Internal Medicine. In 1992, the Joint Commission on the Accreditation of Health Care Organizations (JCAHO) devoted a theme issue of its organ journal, *Quality Review Bulletin*, to defining quality in ethics consultation. In 1993, the Society for Health and Human Values and the SBC collaborated on a report on specialization and certification in ethics consultation.

TRAINING IN ETHICS CONSULTATION

Formal training has been part of ethics consultation for less than a decade. Ethics consultants-in-training can benefit from substantial

Table 2–1   *Early Development of Ethics Consultation*

Programs
> National Institutes of Health
> University of Chicago

Authors
> Fletcher
> Siegler
> Pellegrino
> Jonsen

Literature
> *Clinical Ethics- A Practical Guide*
> *Journal of Clinical Ethics*

Societies
> Society for Bioethics Consultation
> Society for Health and Human Values
> Society for General Internal Medicine
> Joint Commission on the Accreditation of Health Care Organizations

patient care and hospital experience, instruction in case law and legal processes, practice in casuistic moral reasoning and ethical decision making, and knowledge of humanistic behavior. The experience of performing a consultation with a skilled, well-trained mentor, reading carefully about the patient's medical and ethical presentation, and following the patient's case to its conclusion is a practical and traditional process of medical learning. This method of mentorship and follow-up is an integral part of ethics training.

Currently, no universally accepted standards exist for the content of a core curriculum or training program for ethics consultants, although the American Council on Graduate Medical Education has approved a "special ethics track" as part of a geriatric medicine postgraduate fellowship. Most clinical ethics consultants have either a clinical background and ethical training or a philosophical, legal, or theological background and clinical experience. Physicians and nurses generally understand the importance of clinical detail, are comfortable in patient care settings, and speak the language of health care. They are probably best suited to train as ethics consultants. However, philosophers, theologians, and lawyers understand logical analysis and theory, and with sufficient and long clinical training can become very insightful consultants. These consultants can combine the power of their intellectual rigor with a humane approach to the individual patient.

The view that ethics consultants should be clinicians has been criticized in the past, but patients deserve the clinical approach. This is not an attempt to limit the field to physicians and nurses, but rather to insist on a high standard for patient care, which can be met only by those with excellent clinical training and a humane approach to individual patients. If patients are not given good care, it does not matter who is performing the consultation. A consultant must have the ability to acquire and use the necessary skills and to play the appropriate roles of the ethics consultant. Patients and requesting physicians expect the consultant to be specially, clinically prepared.

Who then can train as an ethics consultant? Physicians with broad, primary care backgrounds — internists, family physicians, and pediatricians — are well acquainted with the diversity of cases that ethics consultants are likely to see. Members of other more specialized fields — psychiatrists, gynecologists, surgeons, emergency physicians, and neurologists — can add important perspectives as ethics consultants. Nurses who have an advanced degree and long experience with patients in general or in specialized areas of care are well suited to train as ethics consultants. The complexity of the doctor–patient relationship, the individuality of patients' and families' preferences, goals, and interests, and the exigencies of hospitals, health care professionals, and third-party payers are best appreciated when observed firsthand.

Trainees need some additional education beyond their initial field of expertise (see Table 2–2). For example, trainees need instruction in health law (e.g., relevant case and statutory law regarding life-sustaining treatment, advance directives, and surrogate decision making) and in clinical psychology (e.g., differentiation between organic and functional illnesses and between present and absent decision making capacity). Trainees also need to learn how doctor–patient relationships differ in different medical specialties.

Table 2–2   *Additional Areas of Instruction for Consultants*

- Medical humanism
- Health care law
- Clinical psychology
- Doctor–patient relationships
- Medical sociology
- Ethical reasoning

Table 2–3   *Sample Training Curriculum: Key Courses*

- Case conference
- Illustrative legal cases
- Research in progress
- Reading course
- Journal club
- Narrative ethics

Essential to successful consulting is a clear understanding of the special language, interrelationships, and hierarchies of hospital medicine, nursing, and medical social work. Key courses in a sample training curriculum are suggested in Table 2–3.

Ethics consultants also require some background in ethical reasoning and decision making. Training should provide opportunities to reflect on and critique clinical ethical dilemmas, to discover and discuss multidisciplinary perspectives, and to learn and apply techniques of facilitation and negotiation. Continuing one's primary clinical responsibilities during training is an underappreciated way of discovering ethical dilemmas in patient care.

Ethics Consultation Training Programs

In 1985, only one formal postgraduate fellowship training program existed; there are presently at least ten. The following sections describe the four central training programs that exist. While this list is not exhaustive and is subject to change, these programs model the kinds of training available (see Table 2–4).

The Mid-Career Clinical Apprenticeship Examples include the University of Chicago Hospitals and the University of Virginia in Charlottesville. Training ranges from several months to a full year, and a busy ethics consultation service is required. Indeed, the programs named have among the busiest services in the country. Trainees are practicing clinicians, often physicians and nurses, and may be recruited from within the institution as well as outside of it. The primary objective is to equip established, respected clinicians with the skills to provide discipline- or institution-specific instruction in clinical ethics. Less important than the trainees' potential to assume academic leadership positions is the ability to offer practical, everyday advice. Graduates are expected to return to their own settings and, with assistance, develop and implement programs and practices.

The Postgraduate Fellowship Examples include the University of Chicago Hospitals and Clinics, Loyola University of Chicago, the University of Texas in San Antonio, the Cleveland Clinic Foundation, the University of Minnesota in Minneapolis, the University of Virginia in Charlottesville, the National Institutes of Health, and the University of Florida in Tampa. A one- or two-year training program relies on a knowledgeable, available mentor; rigorous curricular development and adherence; contributions from medicine, economics, literature, law, public policy, philosophy, and theology; and academic sponsorship. Ordinarily, fellows are physicians and nurses

Table 2–4   *Major Training Programs*

- Mid-career clinical apprenticeship
- Postgraduate fellowship
- Graduate degree
- Seasonal seminar

and participate in the hospital ethics consultation service. Philosophers, attorneys, and chaplains may also matriculate. The primary objective is to prepare trainees for academic careers in their primary field, with a specialization in clinical ethics. Graduates are expected to develop educational, service, and research programs in their institutions.

The Graduate Degree Examples include Georgetown University's Kennedy Institute of Ethics, Loyola University of Chicago, Michigan State University in East Lansing, the Medical College of Wisconsin, Rice University in Houston, the University of Texas in Galveston, the University of Pittsburgh's Center for Health Sciences, and the University of Washington in Seattle. The study required ranges from one to six or more years. A consultation service may be available, but participation may not be required. Trainees are usually students of philosophy, ethics, and theology; health professionals may also participate. The primary objective is to train leaders of medical ethics programs for universities and medical schools, who may then compete for research grants and write in the medical, philosophical, or medical humanities literatures. Master's or doctoral degrees may be granted.

The Seasonal Seminar Examples include Michigan State University in East Lansing, the University of Texas in Galveston, the University of Pittsburgh, the Kennedy Institute at Georgetown University, the Midwest Bioethics Center, the University of Washington in Seattle, and Loma Linda University in California. Seminars are generally five days to several weeks long; have structured, rigorous curricula; and are designed to sketch clinical, legal, and philosophical contributions to medical ethics. The programs sometimes require a clinical practicum and usually offer certificates upon completion. Trainees are professionals from many disciplines and often include ethics committee members. Ethics committee members find these seminars very time-efficient, because they do not require protracted periods of study. The primary objective is to provide a grounding in the fundamentals of the field to those unable to matriculate through a formal fellowship. Graduates are asked to complete course materials and often to write a peer-reviewed, graduate-level paper.

THE ETHICS CONSULTANT'S CLINICAL SKILLS

Training programs emphasize a number of key skills (see Table 2–5). These skills enable the consultant to work more productively and effectively. The consultant should be able to identify and analyze ethical problems in a patient's care. The consultant should use reasonable judgment in solving these problems. The consultant should be able to communicate effectively with health care professionals, patients, and families. The consultant should know how to negotiate and facilitate negotiations. Finally, the consultant should be able to teach medical students, house staff, and attending physicians how to identify, analyze, and resolve similar problems in similar cases.

The ability to analyze and separate the ethical questions in a complex case is among the more important skills. In one university hospital series, the consultant identified an average of three ethical issues in each patient's case. The consultation was "very important" or "somewhat important" in clarifying ethical issues in 94 percent of cases.[9] A second important skill, clinical judgment, is difficult to acquire and predicated on experience with many patients and familiarity with the natural histories of many diseases. Judgment underlies effective consultation and equips the consultant to make the casuistic distinctions that are technically and ethically relevant in the care of an individual patient. Attention to the particulars of a given patient's case is the hallmark of good consultation. Particulars vary from one medical specialty to the next; for example, patients and their surgeons have different problems than patients and their emergency physicians.

Table 2–5   *The Consultant's Skills*

- Identifying/clarifying ethical problems
- Demonstrating clinical judgment
- Communicating effectively
- Facilitating negotiations
- Teaching how to construct ethical frameworks

Consultants can teach and model interpersonal skills including listening, reflecting, and encouraging discussion with patients. The consultant should exhibit respect, compassion, and courtesy. Both verbal and nonverbal communication are diagnostic and therapeutic tools and, when carefully developed, practiced, and taught, can directly improve patient care.

The ability to resolve interpersonal conflicts in patient care is an area of special interest for the ethics consultant. Emotionally charged situations that may be identified as ethical dilemmas are more often matters of miscommunication. The consultant should be able to recognize the need for problem solving, whether there are true interpersonal conflicts or communication problems. When administrators or third-party payers are directly involved in a patient care problem, negotiation may take place by telephone, modem, or fax, although these are often poor substitutes for face-to-face interaction.

As a negotiator, the consultant should attempt to find a fair and acceptable solution to a conflict perceived to be an "ethics problem." Often, such a problem is presented to the consultant, even though it may not be concerned with a conflict in values. To solve the problem, the consultant should not necessarily require a consensus, as this may not be possible. The skills of negotiation should allow the consultant to resist any impulse to coerce one party or the other. Negotiation requires an emphasis on common interests instead of on opposing positions, and the use of tact in proposing a patient-centered course of action. The consultant's ability to resolve cases in conflict hinges largely on communication skills.

Finally, the ethics consultant should be able to teach medical students, house staff and attending physicians how to identify, analyze, and help resolve ethical problems. Effective teaching is a learned art; training programs often involve the consultant-in-training in various educational venues, from nursing in-services to ethics committee seminars to medical staff meeings. Each of these may be approached by using a case, reviewing the literature, or adopting a Socratic give-and-take. At minimum, the teacher should have a passion for the subject and a genuine interest in and concern for students. In addition, the consultant's written report can teach through detailed case analysis, with appended references of didactic and practical value. This allows readers to learn in a more formal way how to evaluate their own decision-making framework.

THE ETHICS CONSULTANT'S ROLES

The consultant's possible roles include those of professional colleague, case manager, patient and physician advocate, negotiator, and educator (see Table 2–6). Rather than being a distant and aloof observer of difficult problems, the ethics consultant gets involved and tries to provide help in specific and tangible ways. This help is aimed at improving the outcome of each case.

The ethics consultant is a professional colleague. Rudd describes a professional colleague as "someone with whom to share the case's complexity and from whom discernible help will emerge."[10] Both the ability to analyze ethical issues in a patient's case and the consultant's judgment identify the consultant as a professional colleague. The information, perspective, critique, or reassurance the consultant can provide is tailored to help the requesting physician. As Goldman and colleagues note,[11] the effective consultant is authoritative, independent, collegial and direct.

The ethics consultant is seldom required to manage a patient's case, even when a patient, family, or physician request it. The attending physician should retain decision-making responsibility and authority, using the consultant's ongoing involvement as needed. A consultant does not want to create a dependency among requesting physicians. In addition, this may be construed as "stealing patients," which is always unwelcome. Circumstances may arise, however, where the ethics consultant should be prepared to help manage difficult patients' cases. When a patient's medical interests are threatened or when the primary physician is unavailable or cannot attend to the patient, the consultant may need to intervene in the

Table 2–6   *The Consultant's Roles*

- Professional colleague
- Case manager
- Patient advocate
- Negotiator
- Educator

case. Even in these cases, the consultant's role should be advisory rather than prescriptive.

While the consultant may sometimes make the primary physician's role of medical case manager easier by providing new clinical data and identifying previously unidentified issues, the consultant focuses on helping to resolve the ethical issues in the case and on teaching the physician this skill. Before offering advice, the consultant reviews medical records, interviews and examines patients as appropriate and reasonable, and attempts to discover new data.

When a patient's situation mandates it, the consultant is a patient advocate. The ethics consultant's primary duty is to the patient, although he or she also has duties to the requesting physician. Dual loyalties can be risky for the consultant, especially if he or she opposes the wishes or actions of family members, legal proxies, or physicians. When a patient's interests seem threatened by planned treatment, financial constraints, legal proceedings, or an unreliable proxy, the consultant's obligation may extend to confronting the family or physician, appealing economic constraints, or pursuing legal appeals. Such actions may be difficult and time-consuming, but if harm to the patient seems imminent, the consultant should try to prevent it.

The consultant attempts to assist in the decision-making process as a negotiator when the physician, the patient, or the family requires such assistance. The role of negotiator calls for effective interpersonal and communication skills. As noted earlier, the consultant can try to be a consensus builder, but reasonable people do not always agree on the decisions to be made in a patient's case. Rather, the consultant should help disagreeing parties come to ethically permissible solutions. More often than not, disagreeing parties can come to a practical solution. The role of negotiator may include using persuasion, as ethics consultants have a professional obligation to effect ethically permissible outcomes in their cases.

Finally, the consultant is an educator who teaches the analytic, interpersonal, and communication skills physicians need to solve ethical problems. Teaching ethical decision-making to physicians is a central goal of ethics consultation. The consultant recognizes the requesting physician's ability and experience in analyzing and managing ethical dilemmas, and provides effective, individualized instruction. The consultant then emphasizes principles that may be applicable in similar future cases.

Ethics consultants can anticipate some pressure to assume other roles in the clinical setting. In many cases, however, these roles should be assumed by those individuals with the needed expertise. Ethics consultants may be asked to act as a case conscience (this role usually belongs to all physicians managing the case), case counsel (this role usually belongs to the legal office staff or the patient's attorney), case quality reviewer (this role usually belongs to the quality improvement staff), case psychoanalyst (this role usually belongs to psychiatrists and psychologists), or case clergy (this role usually belongs to hospital chaplains).

Skills and Roles Illustrated: The Nurse Ethicist

The ethics consultant who is a nurse may be uniquely suited to aid in the resolution of ethical dilemmas identified by nurses. The clinical nurse specialist functions as a team member within a defined area of clinical expertise. The clinical nurse specialist is an established role for the advanced nursing practitioner who is skilled as a clinician, consultant, educator, leader, investigator, and change agent. This model of nursing practice is well suited to the nurse who has additional experience and education in clinical ethics.

Primary nurses are often the first to detect an ethical dilemma, and can use their insight and expertise in helping to initiate a formal consultation. In addition, primary nurses can draw on the support, insight, and collaboration of a nurse ethicist who serves as part of a consultation team, with an individual consultant, or as a consultant herself. The following case illustrates one way in which the primary nurse can "call a consult" and use a nurse-ethicist.

Mary Schmitt, RN, was the primary nurse caring for Mrs. Jones, a 92-year-old woman who had been admitted to the hospital with a urinary tract infection and pneumonia. Mrs. Jones had been living in a nursing home for the past seven years, ever since she had a stroke that had left her unable to care for herself. Since that time, Mrs. Jones had two more strokes, had become severely demented, and was now suffering from her third episode of pneumonia in the past six months. Though completely dependent upon others for her needs, Mrs. Jones had, until now, accepted hand feedings and remained fairly well nourished. During this hospitalization, however, Mrs. Jones stopped accepting hand feedings. When food or liquid was placed in her mouth she either allowed the food to drool out or coughed and gagged so forcefully that Mary and other nursing staff had to suction her.

Over the past week, Mrs. Jones's attending physician discussed her worsening nutritional status with her son and daughter. The physician proposed a gastrostomy tube to provide adequate nutrition and hydration. Mrs. Jones's children were reluctant to consent to this. They felt that it would be their mother's wish, under the circumstances, to forego "artificial feeding" of any type. However, Mrs. Jones's physician felt morally and legally obligated to provide nutrition and hydration, because Mrs. Jones had no written advance directives.

After a week attempting to persuade Mrs. Jones's children, the physician documented the emergent need for the procedure, consulted a surgeon who was willing to perform it, and made arrangements with the operating room for the insertion. Mary discussed the issue with Mrs. Jones's physician, and suggested an ethics consultation with the nurse-ethicist. The physician was reluctant. After speaking with her nurse manager and medical director, Mary persuaded the physician to request an ethics consultation.

Nursing has the largest membership of the health care professions, and nurses spend more time in direct patient care than any other group of health care professionals. While many hospitals have forums in which nurses can address ethical dilemmas, many nurses believe that these forums, usually ethics committees, are inadequate. Many critical care nurses, for example, find their strongest support from their nursing colleagues. Nurse managers, nursing supervisors, directors of nursing, and physician staff may provide less support.

The role of the nurse ethics consultant will vary with the institutional setting. The nurse ethicist practicing in a large teaching institution may be part of an ethics consultation service in which two or more consultants share consultation responsibility on a rotational or on-call basis. The nurse ethicist may be part of a consultation team that performs ethics consultations either independently or as a subcommittee of the institutional ethics committee. An independent form of consultation, with telephone referral or backup available, from a consultant colleague is appropriate in institutions (for example, long-term care facilities) where lack of resources or small patient volume does not permit a formal team approach.

As with any consultant, the nurse ethicist's accountability structure must be clearly defined. Reporting channels will depend upon the institutional structure and the institution's goals. If the ethicist is to be primarily a resource to nurses, he or she may report directly to the chief nursing officer. If the ethicist is to serve a wider group of professionals, he or she may report to the institution's administrator. It may be beneficial for the nurse ethicist to apply for professional staff privileges through the medical staff.

However the reporting structure is defined, sponsorship will be vital to the nurse ethicist's success within the institution. The nurse ethicist should be supported by the administration and the nursing and medical staffs. Influential members of these areas should be active in the interviewing and hiring processes. Regularly scheduled feedback sessions from each area should occur in order to identify problem areas.

A nurse ethicist and a physician work well together as a team. The "work" of ethics consultation may be divided or performed jointly, depending upon the needs dictated by the particular case. The nurse consultant often performs much of the data collection, reviewing the medical record and interviewing the patient, staff, and family members as appropriate. The nurse and physician explore the ethical aspects of the case and develop joint recommendations. This may help the patient, as the following case illustrates.

George Lewis is an 84-year-old patient with metastatic lung cancer and COPD. The ethics consultation team was asked to assist in determining whether a "No CPR" or "DNR" order was appropriate for this terminally ill patient who lacked decision-making ability, had no available surrogate decision makers, and did not have a completed advance directive document.

Both the physician and the nurse ethicist went to see Mr. Lewis, who was unresponsive and ventilator-dependent on a monitored, noncritical care unit. The nurse caring for Mr. Lewis informed the consultation team that his blood pressure had been unstable for the past several hours and that his apical pulse rate had dropped into the forties at times. The nurse was maintaining a near-constant presence at the bedside, despite the needs of her other patients. After seeing the patient, the consultation team recommended that a "No CPR" order be written, because CPR held virtually no possibility of efficacy or benefit.

The physician ethicist phoned Mr. Lewis's attending physician, who agreed to write the order and corresponding progress note in a couple of hours. The physician was satisfied with this and felt that the consultation was completed, until the nurse ethicist pointed out that, from the primary nurse's perspective, a two-hour wait may be intolerable. The primary nurse anticipated that cardiac arrest was likely. Once a "No CPR" order was written, the nurse would be free to focus more energy on the comfort of the patient and less on his hemodynamic instability. In addition, more time could be spent with other patients. Based upon this information, the physician telephoned the attending physician again, who requested that the caller write the order.

This case was simple from an ethical standpoint, but it illustrates how nurses and physicians perceive a particular issue differently. It also shows how a nurse and a physician can work together to produce a more comprehensive view of the case.

The nurse ethicist can also provide additional ethics consultation services to nurses about nursing issues. The nurse ethicist should go to the patient care area where the requesting nurse practices, assist the nurse in gathering and clarifying the details of the case, provide the nurse with a framework for problem solving, and help develop specific interventions that will facilitate the resolution of the dilemma.

When appropriate, the nurse can suggest a formal ethics consultation. This may be especially helpful when the identified dilemma involves a physician involved in the case. However, the primary goal of the nursing ethics consultation should be to enable the requesting nurse to address conflict, enhance communication, and negotiate between parties. Recognized formal institutional avenues for addressing problems should be utilized when the dilemma cannot be resolved.

SPECIALIZATION AND CERTIFICATION

The issues of specialization and certification are important for ethics consultants who are interested in pursuing professional development.

Specialization

Several key points support specialization in ethics consultation. First, there is a large body of basic, conceptual research in ethics, published largely in philosophy and history journals, and a growing body of empirical, case-based clinical research, published in medical journals and presented at scientific meetings. Over 3,000 articles and books now appear annually in the field of medical ethics. Second, postgraduate training in medical ethics now exists and employs innovative curricula and formats, which were briefly described in this chapter. Third, most medical schools now have successfully integrated required or elective courses in medical ethics into their didactic curricula. Fourth, ethics questions now appear on the National Boards Step I, II, and Part III, FLEX, the American Board of Internal Medicine's (ABIM) examinations for certification and recertification, and other specialty Board examinations. Fifth, ethics decision-making modules, books, videotapes, seminar series, and special training courses have been developed by professional, educational, and regulation organizations. Sixth, specialization and reimbursement issues are being addressed by organizations of ethics consultants (the American Academy of Medical Ethics, the American Association of Bioethics, and the Society for Bioethics Consultation) and by a medical professional organization (the American Medical Association).

Other political traditions and constituencies, however, do not support specialization. Current key issues include the relatively small number of practitioners, the uncertainty of reimbursement, and the paucity of rigorous evaluations of consultants' performance and effect on patient care. For patient care, specialization has potential advantages and disadvantages. On the one hand, if clinical ethics has a developing special body of knowledge and a clinical process and if its practitioners offer a new, practical expertise, then specialization is one traditional way to recognize, certify, and promulgate these achievements. As a result, institutions may be obligated to make this expertise available as a basic benefit and standard care, to comply with JCAHO and other requirements.

On the other hand, medical care is already overspecialized. Specialization diffuses responsibility for patient care and may further fragment and compartmentalize care, confusing patients and families. Further division of medical care will not enhance patient advocacy or reduce unnecessary treatments. In this view, ethics consultation should be democratized and generalized rather than restricted and specialized. Clinical ethics emphasizes a specialized, rational, and humane decision-making process that all physicians must be able to learn and use.

The American Board of Internal Medicine (ABIM) criteria for a new discipline include the following:

- A significant scientific base and clear-cut relationship to internal medicine or its subspecialties
- A recognition of the discipline in the medical, academic, and scientific communities
- The potential for a significant number of practitioners in a well-defined practice
- A requirement for formal training with prescribed standards
- Improved patient care

With an identifiable scientific knowledge base and improved clinical practice, ethics consultation has begun to meet several of these criteria. While this progress is part of the growth of a field, it seems more like a side effect than a cure. If it helps to improve quality, specialization would be beneficial for patients and practitioners.

Certification

Certification may be warranted for ethics consultation, because a special body of literature, a scientific base, a direct link between clinical ethics and medicine, and preliminary evidence of patient care benefit appear to exist. Clinical ethics is a field of expertise in health care, rather than a separate field, discipline or profession. A separate body of knowledge and special skills are employed by the clinical ethicist who practices effectively. Certification may be useful to protect patients from persons who lack expertise in clinical ethics but who may promote themselves as qualified and credible.

What must a consultant know to be qualified and credible? Drane notes that hospital ethicists should not be too "theoretical, dogmatic, obsessive/compulsive, directive, aggressive, paternalistic and literalistic."[12] It would be difficult to certify these qualities as existing or absent. However, certification may verify that the consultant has proven abilities and an adequate knowledge of the clinical ethics literature as it pertains to patient care. It also may provide payers with a means of appropriately financially recognizing the consultant's time and expertise.

What should be on certification examinations? Physicians may object to examinations that stress philosophical constructs rather than clinical cases. Nonphysician ethicists may object to medically-weighted Board examinations, arguing that nonphysicians exhibit leadership in bioethics. If there are examinations, practical knowledge in medicine, health law, nursing, clinical psychology, and ethical reasoning are critical.

The field of ethics consultation represents a special area of added competence. A notice of added competence, such as the one approved in 1989 in geriatrics, would provide one approach to the validation of this competence and would serve to protect patients from unqualified practitioners. Prior state licensure and Board eligibility (in medicine, for example) would be an initial requirement for such a certificate. Medical licensing acts may cover the licensing of physician ethicists, and this general notion may also cover the scope of ethics consultation services. Continuing education credits would continue to be required in the practitioner's primary field. Nonphysician consultants, such as nurses, may already have licenses to practice in other health care fields. Innovative approaches to certification are especially needed for nonphysician consultants.

With or without formal certification, acceptance of medical ethics as a discipline and ethicists as professional colleagues will still have to be earned, not bestowed. Earning this acceptance will not be easy and will likely depend on the clinical quality of ethics consultations, the academic quality of the foundational and applied research, and on the seriousness and rigor of requirements for certification and licensure.

Because ethics consultants work within highly regulated settings, it is likely that the future will bring regulation to ethics consultation as well. Currently, ethics consultants have a variety of training experiences and a variety of skills. No uniform standard for the training and certification of consultants exists. Generally, if a professional can acquire the necessary clinical skills, see the patient, and gather the appropriate details, that professional can become an ethics consultant, regardless of the certification debate.

CASE CLOSE

In the case of Mark Kennedy the consultant addressed the ethical issues in the case, including the relevance of social worth criteria for expensive, intensive treatment, when and how to break bad news to a patient with cognitive deficits and strong support needs, and how to determine decision-making capacity for treatment and discharge planning.

The consultant noted appropriate medical and penal approaches to Mr. Kennedy's existing alcoholism and motor vehicle violations. Neither problem impacted on the physician's professional obligation to care. The physician and the consultant had agreed that it would have served no humane purpose to tell Mr. Kennedy about the accident while he was critically ill and on mechanical ventilation. Fortunately, and

continued

unbeknownst to the team, Mr. Kennedy's mother had already told him about the accident. On the advice of hospital counsel, the consultant urged Mr. Kennedy's mother to contact the public defender to arrange a defense for her son.

With respect to Mr. Kennedy's "competency" to go to jail, the consultant suggested that the standard of commitment (danger to self or others and mental illness) was more appropriate than that of clinical decision-making capacity (the patient understands and appreciates his or her disease, the treatment offered, and its consequences and alternatives, can make a choice and give a reason). Mr. Kennedy's social worker investigated and found that a nurse was available at the jail 24 hours daily should Mr. Kennedy require medications or treatment. Mr. Kennedy was discharged from the hospital in the sheriff's custody but received appropriate medications and follow-up.

SUMMARY

The recent development of clinical ethics demonstrates that ethics consultation constitutes a distinct professional activity. Ethics consultants find a growing demand for their specialized skills. Empiric studies of ethics consultation are being performed, and journals and professional societies of interest to consultants are proliferating.

The consultant's primary responsibility is to help resolve ethical dilemmas in patient care. This ability to respond to clinical needs builds clinical credibility. Various approaches to consultation are useful. These include the individual consultant, the consultation service and the ethics committee and subcommittee. The legitimacy of ethics consultation is linked to the new and increasing need of patients and physicians for consultation, and to the credibility and accountability of those consultants currently working in the field. A consultant's primary accountability is to individual patients and their physicians, but consultants may also be accountable to institutional bodies, professional associations, and government agencies. A consultant is also accountable to colleagues, institutions, and his or her consultation service.

Ethics consultants should have substantial patient care and hospital experience, instruction in case law, and knowledge of humanistic behavior. The practical aspects of training are greatly enhanced by working with a skilled, well-trained mentor. Ethics consultants usually have clinical backgrounds and ethical training. Various training programs exist, including the mid-career clinical apprenticeship, the postgraduate fellowship, the graduate degree, and the seasonal seminar.

The mid-career clinical apprenticeship program requires several months to a full year of training. An ethics consultation service is usually featured. Trainees are often physicians and nurses.

The postgraduate fellowship program is usually a one- or two-year training that relies on an available mentor and a didactic, practical curriculum. Curricular development is rigorous. Fellows may participate in the hospital ethics consultation service; while they are often physicians or nurses, others may also matriculate. The primary objective is to prepare trainees for academic careers in their primary fields, with a specialization in clinical ethics.

The graduate degree program is a rigorous academic model, requiring one to six or more years to complete. Master's or doctoral degrees are granted. A consultation service may be available, but participation may not be required. Trainees are usually students of philosophy and theology; health professionals may sometimes participate. Most graduates are leaders of medical ethics programs for universities and medical schools and write in the medical, philosophical, or medical humanities literatures.

The seasonal seminar is much less time-intensive than any other training method. Seminars are generally five days to several weeks long, have structured, rigorous curricula, and are designed to sketch out frameworks of clinical, legal, and philosophical approaches to clinical ethics. Trainees often include ethics committee members. The primary objective is to provide some fundamentals for those who are very interested in consultation, but for whom longer, more formal training is unavailable.

The ethics consultant's clinical skills include the ability to identify and analyze moral problems in a patient's case; use reasonable clinical judgment in solving these problems; communicate effectively with health care professionals, patients, and families; negotiate and facilitate negotiations; and teach medical students, house staff, and attending physicians how to identify, analyze, and resolve similar problems in similar cases. The consultant's roles include those of professional colleague, case manager, patient and physician advocate, negotiator, and educator.

Postgraduate training in medical ethics employs innovative curricula and formats. The risks of specialization include the diffusion of patient care responsibility, but the field is becoming specialized, and now requires special training, skills, and roles. Certification and specialization are evolving areas, and the example of how a nurse-ethicist employs some of these skills and roles is illustrative. The future will probably bring some regulation to ethics consultation.

3
Setting Up Practice

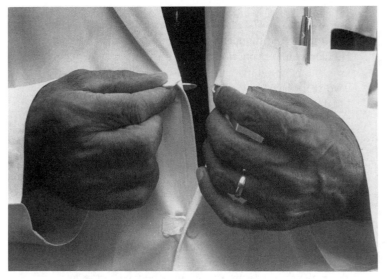

Setting up practice starts with simple things.

The clinical ethicist who wishes to consult faces a number of practical, institutional, and personal issues. These issues are of major concern to a consultant who wishes to perform a significant number of consultations and who also wishes to be paid for this work. The following case will help to illustrate some of the practice issues involved.

Six years ago, a 77-year-old retired executive, Lenny Gordon, was driving in a thunderstorm when a tree fell on his car, knocking him unconscious. He spent the next year recovering from the brain injury, and he moved back home four years ago. Two years ago, Mr. Gordon had a stroke, and his daughter hired a housekeeper for him. Within a year, Mr. Gordon and the housekeeper were married. The daughter applied for guardianship of his estate and person and, soon thereafter, sought and gained the annulment of her father's recent marriage. His recovery from the stroke was slow, and his daughter placed him in a nursing home. For the last six months, Mr. Gordon has had trouble swallowing and walking and has been unable to follow simple commands.

Three months ago, Mr. Gordon's daughter requested a hospice care plan for him, citing "no quality to his life." The medical director of the nursing home agreed and discontinued the patient's antihypertensives and one medication for parkinsonian symptoms. Gastrostomy tube feedings, however, continued and, two months ago, were increased from 75 cc/hour to 90 cc/hour of Jevity. As a result, Mr. Gordon gained weight.

The nursing home, part of a large health care system, did not have a policy concerning the limitation of life-sustaining treatment. Six days ago, the patient pulled out his gastrostomy tube; it was not reinserted because the patient's daughter objected to it and had gone to court to prevent its reinsertion. Legal counsel for the system had been called, and was unsure whether the patient was terminally ill and whether the patient's daughter was a reliable, well-intended proxy.

The consultant went to the nursing home on Saturday, after confirming malpractice insurance coverage and the reimbursement of his time by the long-term care institution. The consultant attempted to interview Mr. Gordon, who was sitting in the dining room. Mr. Gordon held food in the front of his mouth for a long time before swallowing, and he mumbled unintelligibly to the consultant as he did. Mr. Gordon could, however, readily swallow liquid Jevity that the consultant gave him through a straw. The consultant examined him later in his room. Significantly, Mr. Gordon's vital signs were normal, his weight was 145 pounds, and his height was 74 inches. He appeared alert and awake but did not recognize the nurse attending him. He had a right-sided hemiparesis, but his left side was also abnormally rigid and stiff. His skin was intact except for a large Grade I sacral decubitus ulcer.

The consultant interviewed the nursing home administrators ("Thank you for coming"), the nurses caring for Mr. Gordon ("I hope we don't have to put the tube back in"), the medical director ("He is moderately demented, and the tube should have never been put in in the first place"), the dietician ("He has gained weight, but I'll be happy to go along with what the doctor and the family decide"), and the health system legal counsel ("We're adverse here, so I don't want to bias you").

As you can see, setting up practice requires understanding new constituencies and new settings — here, long-term-care providers in a rural nursing home owned by a not-for-profit, nonteaching health system.

Few consultants perform ethics consultations as their primary clinical activity; the vast majority continue their work in their primary field and work on an ethics committee or with an ethics program. Regardless of whether ethics consultation is their primary clinical duty, all consultants will want to consider issues of credibility. Full-time consultants will be especially concerned with writing a job description and finding consultation coverage. Both full-time and part-time consultants will want to know about the following practice issues:

- Establishing credibility
- Writing a job description
- Arranging coverage
- Establishing reporting relationships
- Receiving compensation
- Acquiring hospital privileges for consultation
- Obtaining malpractice insurance
- Evaluating performance
- Keeping up with the literature
- Conducting consultation research

These issues arise differently in different practice settings. This chapter attempts to provide brief, practical discussions of the issues and the settings, and concludes with suggestions for minimizing the stress of ethics consultation.

ESTABLISHING CREDIBILITY

Few standards presently exist against which new, untested, position-seeking ethics consultants can be reasonably measured. In medical practice, accepted standards for new physicians on a medical staff include external factors (where, with whom, and when a physician studied and trained) and personal factors (collegiality and word-of-mouth recommendations from trusted others, including patients, superiors, and peers). In medicine, nursing, and law, the process of state and federal licensure to practice attempts to ensure a minimum professional ability.

Earning credibility without the benefits of licensure and certification (as discussed in Chapter 2) is difficult. It may require special training, extra time, and significant attention to the clinical details of cases in a given institution. The consultant will have to survive within the political milieu of the institution, and some institutions may react slowly, cautiously, and skeptically to new and relatively untested clinical services, especially when there is still only a small possibility of generating revenue with them.

Earning credibility is especially difficult because it is both personal and professional. Besides the skills previously suggested as important, the clinical ethics consultant must demonstrate the four A's: affability, accuracy, availability, and affordability. A consultant who possesses these qualities will become a valued part of the health care institution and medical staff.

Affability, or the ability to get along well with others, requires listening well, inquiring about the cares and concerns of others, and responding respectfully.

Accuracy is a more difficult attribute to acquire, but attention to the diagnosis, prognosis, and treatment as well as the personal, social, familial, and financial aspects of the case can improve the consultant's precision. Consultants should not carelessly relate cases or write poorly formulated notes. Experience is probably necessary for accuracy; following up each case will also improve accuracy. Accuracy is also indirectly reflected by the consultant's penchant for reading, citing, and presenting medical, legal and ethical references.

Availability can be enhanced by following a regular hospital rounding schedule, preferably the same general schedule as most physicians. Similarly, accessibility (by electronic or telephonic means or in visits to the mail room or dining room) permits others to ask informal questions that may not require a formal consultation, and allows the consultant to provide information.

Affordability is the willingness to provide the consultation service at rates consistent with other nonprocedure-oriented, cognitive specialists. Ethics consultation is a basic, time-intensive service, but it is much less expensive than most procedural services provided in clinical settings. In any particular case, one might argue that one of the most cost-effective "procedures" a requesting physician can order is the knowledge and experience that an ethics consultant could bring to a case.

Clinical credibility will have to be earned in a particular clinical culture. Taken altogether, the health care setting has its own rituals, language, and ethos; subcultures within the health care setting (for example, the medical–surgical ward, the rehabilitation center, the burn unit) have their own anthropological traits.

Without a sense of understanding the particular distinguishing traits of a clinical setting, the consultant risks being viewed as an outsider. Moreover, the ethics consultant may be viewed as someone with a negative or condescending attitude toward requesting physicians. Doctor-bashing ethics consultants will fare poorly — their knowledge will be seen as peripheral and their recommendations as overarching and irrelevant.

To earn credibility the consultant should try to attend and, when possible, participate in morning report, mortality and morbidity conference, grand rounds, and attending rounds. The effective consultant understands basic clinical dialect and basically accepts the ethos of medicine: that despite its flaws, medical care exists primarily to help patients get better.

THE JOB DESCRIPTION

Job descriptions form the foundation for a discussion of what the consultant expects to do. In addition, a written job description delineates the interests and objectives of the institution. Institutions may regard the ethics consultant in a number of ways: as a part of the executive management team, as an ad hoc consulting medical staff member with on-call clinical responsibilities, as a visiting educator who teaches residents and students about cases, or as a full-time, hospital-based, clinical employee. The work of four people may also be included in one description, through misguided idealism or simple miscalculation.

Ethics consultants should help write their own job descriptions. If the institution has identified specific responsibilities, it is wise for the consultant and the institutional representative to estimate the hours per week necessary to fulfill each responsibility. The peer-reviewed medical literature on consultation can assist the consultant who wishes to cite an academic source for numbers of hours needed for a given activity. Percentages of the consultant's time, instead of the actual number of hours per week, are unintentionally deceptive — hours per week are more tangible than percentages and do not stop at 100(percent). If the present job description suggests the work of more than one person, the interviewing consultant should either ask permission to amend it to reflect what can reasonably be expected or use the description to advocate for sufficient resources to accomplish the desired tasks. Such resources could provide for an ethics program with colleagues, space, and capital equipment.

In seeking a position in a given institution, the consultant should attempt to match what he or she can offer with what the institution needs. If the consultant is interviewing for a position, it is helpful to meet with key institutional leaders. These people can give the consultant a sense of their (sometimes conflicting) needs and wishes and, later, the type of support available. The consultant can gain even more information about institutional needs by speaking with staff nurses and attending physicians.

CONSULTATION COVERAGE AND BACK-UP

Obtaining back-up coverage is a problem for many medical consultants, especially for solo or rural practitioners. In the only study to report these data, 6 of 30 consultations were judged to be "urgent" by the consultant; in the same study, all patients were seen within a day of request.[1] When the solo ethics consultant is not in the hospital and does not have coverage, requesters may not call back, and the opportunity to serve them will be lost. The consultant may become known as unavailable.

Consultants need trained colleagues. About-to-be hired consultants may wish to suggest that their appointment be conditional on the recruitment of additional help within a reasonable period. Many hospitals will see the wisdom in this suggestion: few want their newly hired expert to burn out. In the academic or university environment, or in institutions where trainees (for example, clinical ethics fellows) or several other persons with ethics consultation privileges take call, a call schedule can be devised with supervisory backup as necessary. Answering machines and the hospital operator can help to direct calls to the on-call consultant.

Without a full-time practice partner, the ethics consultant may wish to limit availability on weekends and at night to emergencies only. When out of town, the consultant should leave a telephone number with the office, answering service, and hospital telephone operators; the consultant should also enlist the help of a reputable and willing colleague in clinical ethics to take urgent calls. The latter approach does entail certain risks; for example, a pinch-hitting consultant may be unaware of the institution's political climate and other such practicalities. The covering colleague is usually required to have temporary consulting privileges, obtained through the chair of his or her clinical department and the medical staff office, and to bring his or her own malpractice coverage as well. Appropriate remuneration and temporary staff privileges for an outside consultant for a particular case can be part of the ethics consultant's contractual arrangement with the hospital. Even when two consultants practice in the same setting (usually the best circumstance, in that they can cover for each other), their personal and other professional duties may not allow for full-time coverage.

If the demand for service overwhelms a consultant's ability to act competently, the consultant should notify his or her sponsors, and make suggestions for action. These may include hiring a colleague, utilizing the political and administrative support of an ethics committee, or borrowing the resources and expertise of a nearby ethics center. Sponsorship will be discussed in more detail in the next section.

If the consultant succeeds in gaining sufficient hospital and medical staff support, he or she may be able to secure sufficient resources to train clinical colleagues as a future means of providing coverage. Securing sufficient resources can be difficult, but creative approaches may bring them about where there seemed to be only interest. Clinical colleagues in ethics may emerge from within the institution; once trained, the consultant can assist them in obtaining staff privileges. Ethics consultation practices have been organized as group practices and even as legal firms, working under the protective umbrella of staff privileges. Relatively few consultants, however, will have the opportunity to provide for consultation coverage by training colleagues themselves, because the resources required for a training program may be out of reach for many institutions.

REPORTING RELATIONSHIPS

As discussed in Chapter 1, the consultant's primary accountability is to the patient and the requesting physician. Most of the time, the patient and the physician have the same fundamental needs, interests, and goals. When their interests conflict, however, the consultant should work to protect the patient's interests. In this sense, the consultant "reports to" the patient first and foremost.

At another level, the consultant must work within the same web of complex reporting relationships as do other clinical consultants. Section heads, department chairs, medical staff officers, institutional leaders, professional credentialing bodies, and state licensing authorities are some of those to whom the consultant may report; between and among these people, consultants may have multiple, overlapping, and occasionally conflicting loyalties.

Consultants are usually employees with contractual responsibilities to their institution and primary sponsor. Sponsorship can be thought of as support from effective, authoritative, and powerful institutional sources. Effective sponsorship can provide the consultant with the resources necessary to do the job and with a way of making sure that ideas for improvement and innovation are implemented as part of an established institutional process. Sponsorship is also important for the consultant who makes potentially unpopular recommendations. Sponsors can also reward the good performance of the ethics consultant and provide future guidance. In general, hospital ethics consultants whose duties are primarily ethics should report to and be primarily sponsored by a top manager in the health care institution—a chief executive officer, a chief medical officer, a medical staff president, a medical school or university dean, or an associate dean for academic affairs. Consultants whose primary duties lie in another field may be primarily sponsored by the top manager in that field—a department chairperson, for example.

A reporting relationship to a top manager is usually advantageous, because it can make the consultant more accessible to physicians in many departments. The manager may also support special educational efforts or research projects with which the consultant requires assistance.

COMPENSATION AND BILLING

Compensation is one of the most controversial areas in ethics consultation. Some feel that consultation should never be done on a fee-for-service basis; others think that consultants should bill by the hour, as do many attorneys in private practice. One possible way of determining fair compensation is to describe what others with the same types of credentials are paid for their work. Fellowship-trained specialists in medicine, for example, are paid at least 25 percent more than those without fellowship training. Chairmen of clinical departments are paid more than most members of those departments. Private practitioners are paid more than academicians, and procedurally oriented specialists are paid more than cognitively oriented generalists. Clinical nurse specialists are paid 35–70 percent of what physicians are paid. The only doctoral professionals to be paid for clinical care are licensed clinical psychologists, who make about 80 percent of what psychiatrists make. Compensation also varies by region of the country, size of the town, and practice setting.[2]

Ethics consultants are currently paid in several different ways (see Table 3–1). They may be salaried in full or in part by health care institutions to provide hospital-based service; by large multispecialty medical groups to provide fee-for-service consultation; or by health care systems to provide advice to corporate management and member hospitals, nursing homes, and other treatment centers. Consultants may be part of private practice groups; some of these contract with clients (for example, health care systems, managed care organizations, hospitals, or medical groups) to provide ethics consultative services at hourly rates. Private practice consultants in these groups may receive a base salary, an educational allowance, and even incentive bonuses, all based on mutually agreed upon goals.

Table 3–1   *Compensation Options for Ethics Consultants*

- Salaried faculty, institutionally based
- Salaried member, multispecialty group
- Salaried member, managed care organization(s)
- Fee-for-service, partnership
- Fee-for-service solo practice
- No direct compensation for clinical service

Unfortunately, many ethics consultants do not receive direct remuneration for their consultation activity and serve as full-time or part-time faculty in teaching institutions, donating their consultative services to institutions, colleagues, families, and patients. Because consultation requires a significant investment of the consultant's (and others') time, it is unlikely that these pro bono arrangements will continue much longer. Individuals and institutions are increasingly cost conscious, and some method of cost recovery will be important both to those who wish to make (part of) their living consulting and to those who wish to keep their institutions financially afloat.

An unfair trade on the consultant's need for compensation, however, may increase revenue but will decrease integrity and professionalism. For example, some health care institutions have asked ethics consultants to try to save money for them by evaluating the care of patients whose hospital course has been especially costly. Institutional pressures that force the ethics consultant to adopt the role of cost cutter are likely to increase, as institutional leaders become more aware of the consultant's ability to elicit and evaluate patient preferences, especially those preferences to avoid life-sustaining treatment near the end of life.

But what's wrong with saving the institution money and working to avoid undesired treatment? Analyzed and attended to openly, explicitly, and separately, nothing is wrong with them.

Conflating concerns about death and dying or quality of life with concerns about cost containment, however, represents a personal conflict of interest for the consultant, whose own needs, desires, and values may be too easily compromised by such an arrangement. Although cost-effectiveness data may be important to institutions and payers, it is not the primary fulcrum on which compensation for ethics consultation rests. Instead, the consultation's quality, including the consultant's effectiveness in promoting better communication, advancing patient goals, and helping to teach physicians and others to make their own decisions, are identifiable and logical measures for compensation.

Ethics consultation, however, is not lucrative. Even if ethics consultation becomes part of an accepted benefits package, and consultants are hired by managed care organizations and indemnity insurers, it is unlikely consultants will be able to generate enough in patient care revenues to meet their salary requirements.

Most consultants do not presently bill by the hour, and no procedure code or diagnostic category currently exists just for ethics consultation. Still, an appropriate CPT code for the type of consultation performed and an appropriate ICD-9-CM code for the diagnosis made may be assigned. Often, the consultation involves a family conference, and the appropriate CPT code may acknowledge such participation.

As in other clinical areas, success in collecting billings seems to correspond directly with promptness in submitting the bill; resubmitting bills, if rejected, often results in their payment. Third-party payers of all types — Medicare, Medicaid, managed care organizations, and indemnity insurers — have paid for ethics consultations. Some insurers may pay bills only when a physician assigns an appropriate medical diagnosis and performs and signs the consultation, utilizing an ethics consultation protocol. Whether a medical degree is necessary for this sort of insurer-based reimbursement is unknown. In the meantime, consultants will continue to create, participate in, and try out innovative arrangements for seeing patients.

Billing at the community prevailing rate for subspecialty, non-procedure-oriented medical consultation (for infectious disease, for example) seems reasonable, and professional organizations have begun to take steps to seek appropriate reimbursement for consultants. The American College of Physicians' 1992 ethics manual notes that consultation can be helpful to physicians struggling with difficult cases. Also in 1992, the American Medical Association's Council on Medical Services suggested that third-party payers seriously consider full reimbursement for ethics consultations that provide clinical services, including detailed medical and historical, examination, and decision-making documentation. As we go to press, the AMA's House of Delegates is scheduled to debate whether to call on managed care organizations and the Health Care Financing Administration for compensation for ethics consultants.

Finally, inexperienced consultants may confuse what they need to work and set up their programs (resources) and what they need to live (compensation). Resources include the possibility of obtaining colleagues and secretarial support, as well as tuition coverage or other benefits. Hays and Associates and AAMC surveys have helped determine the consultant's peer group: Hays has developed a compensation evaluation for clinical ethicists.[3] Most importantly for the beginning consultant, sufficient resources and compensation must be guaranteed to permit the consultant to work effectively.

HOSPITAL PRIVILEGES

Obtaining hospital privileges for consultation from hospital trustees requires permission from the medical staff. In some teaching hospitals, particularly those directly affiliated with universities, the medical staff's authority is derived from the department chair, the hospital president, or the medical school dean. In this setting, the privileges committee of the medical staff is adjunctive, and new departmental faculty are almost uniformly given privileges by the hospital. This is especially important for ethics consultants; if they are recruited by the dean or the chair of a clinical department, they will have a powerful ally who can then help them obtain consultation privileges.

In most community hospitals, the medical staff takes more initiative in and control of the privileges process and may exclude persons who request privileges. The privileges committee may even (unofficially) regulate the number of practitioners who are able to apply for privileges in a given specialty or discipline. This committee is also interested in improving the standard of care in the institution and sometimes may try (despite antitrust concerns) to minimize competition.

Especially in community hospitals, establishing the need for ethics consultation (for example, by documenting informal requests for consultation over a particular period of time) and having the support and sponsorship of the medical staff president and the hospital president can be essential in obtaining privileges. The ethics consultant may need an advocate or several advocates on the committee to testify on behalf of the consultant's training, skills, and abilities. In rare cases, clinical ethics may already have divisional or departmental status, and the consultant can apply for privileges under the aegis of that department; more commonly, the consultant will be able to apply for special privileges in clinical ethics in his or her primary clinical department.

The JCAHO requires its members to have a mechanism for assisting in " . . . the resolution of moral dilemmas in patient care."[4] To comply with this requirement and to protect patients from persons who lack expertise in ethics, but who may promote themselves as qualified ethics consultants, consultation privileges have been suggested. Clinical privileges routinely include evidence of current licensure, relevant training or experiences, board certification or eligibility, and demonstrated competence. One model for clinical privileges for ethics consultation is based on a detailed review of the policy statements of major professional organizations in internal medicine, family practice, pediatrics, psychiatry, and other major specialty organizations, and on the evaluation of data from the ethics consultation literature and from major training programs in clinical ethics.[5]

It is possible for practitioners who are not physicians to be admitted to medical staffs and to enjoy the protective institutional rubric that clinical privilege standards provide. The Health Care Financing Administration has suggested "Doctoral Professional" as a new category for medical staffs. Such categories may appropriately accommodate nonphysician ethicists who otherwise meet the delineated criteria for privileges. For example, standard criteria for medical privileges may be modified to include appropriately trained, experienced, and licensed nurses with, at minimum, a master's degree; appropriately clinically trained and experienced philosophers and theologians with a doctoral degree; and attorneys, allied health professionals, and others willing to seek and undergo the appropriate clinical training and experience, and gain recognition by state licensing bodies.

For practical purposes, Table 3–2 shows model for a delineation of staff privileges when the consultant is a physician ethicist; Table 3–3 shows a model for a delineation of staff privileges when the consultant is not a physician ethicist. Although these models are similar, important differences exist between the credentialing and licensing requirements of physicians and other professionals. These models attempt to reflect those differences, which were also discussed briefly in Chapter 1.

Clinical privileges will not be guaranteed to every consultant who presents himself or herself, but will likely be necessary for ethics consultants in acute and long-term care institutions. Consultants who are inexperienced and only beginning to develop expertise, or who have not completed a postgraduate fellowship, may be awarded

Table 3–2   *Staff Privileges in Clinical Ethics: An Institutional Model (Discipline-Specific): Physician-Ethicists*

I. A degree (M.D. or D.O.) from an accredited medical college.

A. Current in-state licensure to practice medicine in good standing.

B. Board certification in an American Board of Medical Specialities medical discipline.

C. Completion of at least one year full-time, or equivalent, of a formal postgraduate fellowship training program in clinical ethics.

D. Documentation of at least 25 supervised, directly performed consultations, preferably while in fellowship training.

E. Demonstration, through peer-reviewed publication and the recommendation of an applicant's supervisor, of the adequacy of the applicant's skills, including the ability to "identify and analyze ethical problems in a case, use reasonable clinical judgment, communicate effectively, negotiate and facilitate negotiations, and teach others how to construct their own decisionmaking frameworks."*

*J. LaPuma and E.R. Priest, "Medical Staff Privileges for Ethics Consultants: An Institutional Model," *Quality Review Bulletin* 18, no. 1 (1992): 17–20.

temporary or conditional privileges, or they may be asked to work with the legal department, the ethics committee, or an outside authority in the field. Malpractice insurance and compensation mechanisms can be considered a part of the discussion regarding privileges and are considered further in the following sections.

MALPRACTICE PREVENTION

The question of an ethics consultant's legal liability has been addressed on theoretical grounds, but no known suit has yet been brought against an ethics consultant for his or her analysis or advice. The effect of such a suit could be negative and chilling in a new field like ethics consultation. The only suit brought against an ethics committee (High Desert Hospital's decision in Elizabeth Bouvia's case) resulted in that committee's dormancy for nearly four years, despite dismissal of the suit without award in 1990. The idea that an

Table 3–3   *Staff Privileges in Clinical Ethics: An Institutional*
Model (Discipline-Specific): Nonphysician-Ethicists

I. A postgraduate degree from an accredited institution.

   A. Current in-state health professional licensure or other legal
     credential required by state law (for example, to practice nursing or
     law) in good standing. If inapplicable (for example, for
     philosophers), individual arrangements may be negotiated.

   B. Completion of at least one year full-time, or equivalent, of a formal
     postgraduate fellowship training program in clinical ethics.

   C. Documentation of at least 25 supervised, directly performed
     consultations, preferably while in fellowship training.

   D. Demonstration, through peer-reviewed publication and the
     recommendation of an applicant's supervisor, of the adequacy of
     the applicant's skills, including the ability to "identify and analyze
     ethical problems in a case, use reasonable clinical judgment,
     communicate effectively, negotiate and facilitate negotiations, and
     teach others how to construct their own decisionmaking
     frameworks."*

*J. LaPuma and E.R. Priest, "Medical Staff Privileges for Ethics Consultants: An Institutional Model," *Quality Review Bulletin* 18, no. 1 (1992): 17–20.

ethics consultant can be negligent or commit malpractice implies that he or she has a specific duty that can be breached, that the breach can be measured against the standard of care, and that the breach can cause demonstrable patient injury, harming the patient.

Whether consultants can be held negligent depends in large part on whether they meet the standard of care—a complex, evolving notion that turns on technical knowledge, legal constraints, and judgment. At present, there is no malpractice coverage specifically for ethics consultation, nor, as previously noted, is there any claims experience. Many consultants are covered under the same claims coverage as staff physicians; this makes the privileges issue very important.

Malpractice prevention is integrated in the careful approach to patient cases that has been outlined. Clear documentation of dates, times, places, and interactions in a particular case, with quoted statements when possible, is part of malpractice prevention. The consultant has a professional obligation to assist requesting physicians in identifying and analyzing key ethical dilemmas in a particular case. Unless there is a blatant and critical ethical issue that is not part of the question asked, the legal obligation extends only to answering the question that is asked. Answering the question clearly, suggesting options instead of writing orders, and reading and referencing appropriate and up-to-date literature support the consultant's opinion.

One way to reduce liability concerns and malpractice worries is to recognize the limits of one's own training. It is also helpful to consult freely with colleagues and other experts. Consulting with hospital attorneys is advisable in cases where legal issues are prominent or highly controversial. The law is a dynamic body of knowledge and opinion, with as many shadings, controversies, interpretations, and uncertainties as medicine. Legal colleagues suggest that compared to obstetricians, gynecologists, and orthopedists, ethics consultants generally have little to worry about. Consultants who are especially concerned about lawsuits may find beneficial an ethics consultation service comprised of a physician-ethicist, a nurse, and an attorney.

Malpractice Insurance

For physician ethicists who have faculty appointments in hospitals or who join medical groups, malpractice insurance commensurate with that of other medical subspecialists (at least $1,000,000/$3,000,000) should be a condition of employment. Often, malpractice insurance is provided as part of institutional employment. As an extra precaution, some consultants ask the insurer to provide a special insurance rider for ethics consultation in addition to one for medical duties.

Consultants in private consultation practice can obtain malpractice insurance privately, or they may assure that the institution for which they consult will extend coverage. Nonphysician ethicists will usually be required to show evidence of plans for malpractice coverage with their medical staff applications; they may be able to obtain coverage through the medical staff office and its contacts. Alternatively, nonphysician ethicists may be invited to join an institution or medical group whose insurance will cover them for professional negligence.

EVALUATION OF ETHICS CONSULTANTS

Annual evaluation of the consultant's performance may help the institution or group to determine whether compensation adjustments, position changes, and special quality improvement are needed. An evaluation may also permit the consultant to shape mutually agreed upon short- and long-term goals.

Performance evaluation criteria might include whether the consultant demonstrates in a quantifiable way the roles of professional colleague, negotiator, patient and physician advocate, case manager, and educator. Performance evaluation is usually tied directly to an employee's job description, which should be carefully crafted by the consultant in conjunction with the institution. Secondary evaluative standards include achievement of institutional goals and the consultant's personal goals. If the consultant's skills and roles can be defined clearly in behavioral terms, the evaluation might be conducted in these terms.

Alternatively, an outside expert may provide a subjective peer evaluation. Evaluating the quality of educational presentations, perhaps using before/after surveys, and testing the consultant's degree of familiarity with clinical, legal, and ethics journals might also be helpful. The institution may be able to assess the consultant's demonstration of the four A's (affability, accuracy, availability, and affordability). However, if the consultant is to be evaluated using these axioms, their mutually agreed-upon quantification before any assessment is desirable. Criteria that should not be used for evaluation of consultant performance include the amount of money he or she has saved the hospital, the length of written consultations, or the number of references provided per consultation.

Favorable evaluations may bring promotion. In many academic medical centers, including hospitals that are affiliated with medical schools, rank and tenure committees may focus on how many publications and how much grant money the consultant has produced. Even in institutions with clinician–educator tracks, the ethics consultant may have to produce these types of accomplishments to gain promotion or increased compensation. Consultants who create new programs, sections, divisions, or even departments may be compensated based on the success or failure of these achievements. In general, successes are financially self-sufficient.

Finally, evaluation of clinical competence in ethics consultation may be formalized by means of a written or oral examination or other quantitative and qualitative assessment. As discussed in Chapter 2, a certificate of added clinical competence may be helpful in ensuring that the consultant has the minimum standard of knowledge and ability required to consult effectively.

KEEPING UP

The consultant can often find well-researched, persuasive articles that support diametrically opposing points of view in any given case. Although requesting physicians usually want practical answers as opposed to evenhanded explorations of the current controversy, they may appreciate hearing both points of view and seeing these articles.

What material does the consultant read? Large volumes exploring ethical theories, virtues, or theology? Current medical and scientific abstracts, which may reveal advances in innovative treatment and research findings? Computer compilations of abstracted "ethics" articles in different published literatures? Handbooks of clinical ethics designed to fit in an intern's pocket? *The New York Times?* Consultants may read all of these, but first and foremost, they should read about their cases. This includes pertinent major medical, legal, philosophical, or theological sources. Consulting an expert for references, searching professionally prepared annotated bibliographies of ethics (increasingly specialty specific), and examining key journals are helpful strategies for reading about a case. Interactive video programs are just being developed to allow learners to work their way through a case.

Sometimes, a search of a comprehensive computer data base, such as MEDLARS or COLLEAGUE, is helpful in finding the most recent medical information to address a specific question that has an evolving answer (for example, What is the current survival of AIDS patients with respiratory failure on a ventilator?). BIOETHICSLINE is also occasionally helpful in patient cases.[6]

General reading for the consultant minimally consists of key journals, such as *New England Journal of Medicine, Annals of Internal Medicine, Journal of the American Medical Association, Hastings Center Report* and *Journal of Clinical Ethics).* Other general reading sources include the journals and ethics publications of major professional societies, such as the JCAHO, the American Medical Association, the American College of Physicians, the American Academy of Pediatrics, the American College of Obstetrics and Gynecology, and the American Academy of Family Practice.

In addition, consultants who work primarily in one or two specific fields should be familiar with the literature from those specialty bodies. Relevant state and federal case and statutory law are useful reading, as are copies of major legal opinions in health care law. Medical libraries often have most of these materials, and local law school libraries or state legal societies can supply the specialized legal materials. Adequate electronic and video sources of continuing ethics education are still largely unavailable, but this situation is improving. To capture a broad sampling of this material, some consultants start ethics journal clubs, inviting colleagues in different health care specialties and subspecialties to present a key ethics article each month. Conferences abound in ethics, but few to date have focused on maintaining or improving consultation practice.

CONSULTATION RESEARCH

Ethics consultation research has centered on the consultation's content, promptness, educational utility, and clinical assistance, and employed the conceptual methods of philosophy, theology, law, and public policy, as well as the empirical methods of clinical practice, the social sciences, decision analysis, clinical epidemiology, and health services research. Consultation research produces and disseminates knowledge through scholarly publication and has described patient cases, requesters' and ethics consultants' reasons for consultation, requesters' evaluations of a university hospital's and a community hospital's consultation services, and the importance of medical indications, patient preferences, quality of life, and socioeconomic factors in decision making in patient cases.

Few empiric data are available about hospital ethics consultation, its different methods, or the results of ethics consultation. In Chapter 1, we reviewed briefly several studies of consultation outcomes. A National Institute of Health (NIH) survey of ethics consultants found that 43 percent of the respondents regularly wrote in patient records[7] and received an average of seven formal consultations annually. Sixty-five percent of university physicians requesting an ethics consultation of a physician ethicist working with an ethics committee said that the consultant should be available after hours, have medical ethics training, and speak directly with the requester.[8] A prospective evaluation of a university ethics consultation service found that requests for consultations were evenly distributed through the different days of the week, and focused on cases in the intensive care unit.[9]

Many evaluative descriptive data do exist. A clinical approach to ethics consultation that uses a teaching service staffed by a trained physician ethicist has successfully provided clinical and educational value in at least two settings—a university hospital and a private community teaching hospital. When both conceptual and empiric methods are used, especially fruitful research can occur. The effect of long-standing doctor–patient relationships on decision making, the components of physicians' personal value systems, and the setting in which the consultation is conducted may influence the consultation's helpfulness should be studied.

Because process and outcome are often intertwined, some of the components of consultation are difficult to measure and evaluate. Even without access to an ethics center, the consultant, or a medical sociologist or a health services researcher, can describe the actions and interactions of those involved in a difficult case, attempt to define what made it difficult, and explain why it was difficult for the benefit of colleagues. Detailed case analysis is a time-honored tradition in medicine, and it is probably also the most basic and accessible form of ethics consultation research.

PRACTICE SETTINGS

Ethics consultants work in a variety of practice settings, and in each setting, the consultant strives to understand the demands of the specific milieu and the special needs of those who ask for assistance. A number of these settings, including teaching, nonteaching, community, for-profit, long-term care, and rural institutions will be discussed in the following sections.

Teaching Hospitals

Ethics consultants in teaching hospitals have the dual responsibilities of educating students and house staff and caring for patients. Most often, these consultants are full-time faculty of the medical school with which the hospital is associated. Usually, such consultants are deeply involved with and may even be sponsored by university-affiliated ethics centers. Often, these ethicists are active in teaching house staff as well, and this interaction with medical students and house staff provides an extensive teaching and referral network. Ethics consultants in teaching institutions have the special opportunity to model clinical ethics for students in daily clinical interactions.

In teaching hospitals, a clinical ethics consultation program may contribute to the institution through patient service activities, broad scale teaching programs, and management assistance. Specific contributions include:

1. The development of teaching programs in medical ethics for attending medical staff, house staff, nurses, and other caregivers
2. The development of a service that can provide assistance in patient care
3. The participation in, chairing of, or helping to develop an institutional ethics committee (IEC) and network
4. Service as a liaison or advisor (on medical ethics and related legal issues) to the medical–legal office, the hospital or system president, and the board of trustees
5. The research and sharing of answers to important clinical questions using prospective and retrospective empiric studies, clinical case analyses, and conceptual research presented in peer-reviewed settings.[10]

Institutions with strong, professionally accomplished, scholarly ethics centers are also likely to attract media attention. The media often request interviews on important technological, social, and professional developments. Many ethics consultants accept such opportunities, because they represent creative ways to promote the institution's innovative approach to ethical dilemmas.

University teaching hospitals and community teaching hospitals differ in several ways. In university hospitals, consultations are often aimed primarily at house staff, with minimal patient care direction or formal attending physician interaction. The ethics consultant may send a resident or student currently on an ethics elective to gather the details of a case and report back. Thus, the case can become a highly effective resident-to-resident interaction with attending staff overview. In community teaching hospitals, however, the consultant is nearly always called personally by the primary attending and often handles some, and sometimes all, data gathering, as the emphasis in many community teaching hospitals is primarily on clinical service and secondarily on teaching trainees. In both the university and the community setting, the consultant may choose to handle a case personally when it is extraordinarily complicated or delicate.

Nonteaching Community Hospitals

Less is known about the role of the consultant in nonteaching hospitals. These are important future settings for ethics consultation, because most patients are hospitalized in nonteaching community hospitals. In 1989, the American Hospital Association found only eight ethics centers based in community hospitals, all of which were teaching hospitals. Thus, to reach more patients and physicians, ethics consultants are beginning to consider working in nonteaching community hospitals.

As part of their institutional mission, nonteaching institutions are interested in the continuing education of their staff. Indeed, as in teaching hospitals, the hospital's values and mission statement can include a focus on clinical ethics. The ethics consultant's teaching role is still important in the nonteaching community hospital, but the nature of the teaching is different. Instead of ethics fellows, house officers, and medical students, the consultant's audience is staff physicians, nurses, families, and patients. The health professionals require education about problem solving and recent developments in literature and health care law. Patients and families care first that they are taken care of well by their personal physician, and care second about everything else. The education is more informal and less didactic than in teaching hospitals, and the ethics consultant is seen as a clinical resource and colleague rather than as a professor.

In the nonteaching hospital, the ethics consultant, like his or her colleagues, is primarily a practitioner. Initially, requesting physicians may test the consultant's mettle and ability with a difficult but well-defined case. Especially in the nonteaching hospital, the ethics consultant must prove he or she can handle such cases before expecting to be consulted on more difficult, more complex cases. Such cases, perceived as impossible to resolve, may involve heated conflict or disagreement among the staff. In these cases especially, it is essential that the ethicist avoid presumptuousness and suppress any reformist tendencies.

Measuring oneself by quantity rather than quality is a common pitfall for consultants in nonteaching settings. Building a busy, growing practice is the goal of many practitioners, and, like these colleagues, the consultant's success may be often measured by the number of patients he or she is asked to see, the number of hospitals in which he or she has consulting privileges, or his or her net patient care income. Primarily, the ethics consultant should gauge success by the quality of work rather than the sheer quantity of consultations. Ethics cases are complex, and a full-time consultant may be able to do high-quality work on only four or five cases a week. In this sense, ethics consultation is more like a comprehensive geriatric consultation than a focused dermatology consultation.

Ethics consultants presently work in several nonteaching settings, three of which deserve special consideration.

Freestanding, For-Profit Hospitals "For profit" is a tax designation. Some commentators note that all hospitals are for-profit, since "not-for-profit" or "tax-exempt" hospitals simply distribute earnings to research and development instead of to shareholders or staff. Others think there is a difference, because the explicit mission of for-profit institutions is to make money. Their employees are expected to help them achieve that goal, and the resulting pressure on the nursing and medical staff may result in shorter lengths of stay or higher occurrence of illness at discharge. It does appear, however, that not-for-profits now resemble for-profits in their marketing programs and in some of their medical and financial behaviors.

In a for-profit environment, the consultant gathers data in the usual way, but he or she must develop several other dimensions of analysis when seeing a patient. The consultant should keep institutional integrity and faithfulness in mind during consultation just as he or she would in a not-for-profit institution. A for-profit institution's financial goals are not necessarily malevolent or badly intentioned, and top management, which is often no different than in a tax-exempt institution, may regard running a hospital as a moral enterprise with socially accountable mission, vision, and values. To act on its moral agency, the institution may want to consider, for example, the results of the consultant's research on the influence of the institution's financial goals on his or her recommendations for patient care. The consultant may also propose institutional policies that ameliorate potential financial conflicts of interest. The consultant may even be able to help the institution clarify its mission with regard to the need for separating clinical ethics and revenue generation.

One recorded attempt at this clarification follows. A consultant was asked to comment on the ethical issues raised by a proposed for-profit research venture at a not-for-profit community hospital.[11] Indigent patients would have been excluded from the research, which offered an expensive experimental medication for renal cell carcinoma and melanoma that was reportedly about to be approved by the FDA. In response, the consultant prepared a specific proposal, identifying dilemmas of informed consent, conflict of interest, and discrimination. The consultant persuaded the hospital administrators to pay heed to several ethical principles, and suggested particular changes in the research protocol that otherwise would not have been considered. As a result, these changes were incorporated in the protocol, and indigent patients were included. While not every story will have such an ending, consultants can assist for-profits in fostering and encouraging a sense of moral accountability beyond a financial bottom-line mentality.

Long-Term Care Facilities The complexity of geriatric medicine, the mechanisms of payment for long-term care, and the changing definitions and parameters of doctor–patient–family relationships make ethics consultation in long-term care facilities especially challenging. Most physicians make infrequent rounds in long-term care facilities; Medicare currently only pays for monthly visits. Increased reimbursement for discussions of complex decision-making has not been fully realized. Thus, physicians are at the patient's side much less often than nurses, who often assume leadership roles in ethical and clinical decision-making.

In long-term care, the ethics consultant will commonly encounter dilemmas of patient autonomy. Many residents fear the loss of personal choices, especially ones that involve basic activities of daily living. Death and dying issues are often keenly important to elderly patients, as are health care costs, which are usually paid for privately at first. Most residents of Medicaid homes have spent any savings to gain nursing home admission. The consultant may also encounter estranged families and find nurses and nurses' aides who pay closer attention to patients than do family members. These nurses and aides may become surrogate family members, and may be able to assist in decision-making for their charges. Fearing a conflict of interest, not all states, however, allow residents to name their caregivers as health care proxies.

Consultation staff privileges in long-term care facilities can usually be arranged through the nursing home administrator. Most facilities are not teaching facilities per se. However, several innovative programs focusing on ethical issues in long-term care facilities have been developed. They include the video monitoring of residents at risk for falls, rather than the use of mechanical restraints; policies governing the treatment of patients with Stage IV pressure sores; and "personal value assessments" on admission, including optional completion of a written advance directive.

Rural Hospitals Consultants who work in nonteaching rural hospitals may face pressing issues of isolation, triage, confidentiality, and privacy. Rural professionals are sometimes frustrated by their inability to access a major medical center when patients need tertiary access and high technology. Contrary to popular myth, rural clinicians face the same clinical dilemmas as do urban clinicians. Many difficult problems, including emergency triage, for example, arise in a busy rural emergency room on a Saturday night. In addition, the ethics consultant may find that rural physicians struggle with conflicting personal and professional truth-telling obligations: confidentiality and privacy can be in short supply in communities where everyone knows everyone else. For example, while a physician has a legal duty to report a positive serologic test for syphilis to public health authorities, this can be difficult when the patient is one's own medical office employee, a prominent community member, or an official in local government.

Many small communities and rural hospitals are unable to support a full-time ethics consultant, so the consultant also practices in his or her primary field more than does his or her urban counterpart. The rural ethics consultant, like the rural family doctor, learns to be self-sufficient. Personal access to colleagues is limited, but fortunately technology (cellular telephones, modems, and fax machines) and centers of excellence (some urban clinical ethics centers) have diminished some of this isolation. These resources may be even more important to rural consultants than they are to urban practitioners.

PERSONAL STRESS

Ethics consultants, like other professionals, can be subject to burnout or impairment. Burnout is described by the AMA as the "process by which a once committed health professional becomes ineffective in managing the stress of frequent emotional contact with others in the helping context, experiences exhaustion, and as a result disengages from patients, colleagues, and the organization."[12] The burned-out professional becomes apathetic and critical of others. Common professional responses to burnout include less time spent with patients, tardiness, absenteeism, medication errors, poorly charted observations, impersonal or stereotyped communication with patients, a search for relocation, and inefficient patient care.

Burnout can lead to impairment. The AMA defines an impaired physician as one "unable to practice medicine with reasonable skill and safety to patients because of physical or mental illness, including deteriorations through the aging process or loss of motor skill, or excessive use or abuse of drugs including alcohol."[13] Impairment has also been defined as the end of a stress continuum, which progresses from normal to increased stress to burnout to impairment.

If ethics consultants have earned a good clinical reputation, their clinical success can also be their undoing. The shortage of colleagues may promote an increased reliance on a consultant as the only resource available. Overloaded with poorly controllable demands on his or her time, the consultant may find it difficult to juggle other priorities, such as personal, family, and spiritual needs. Indeed, the

Table 3–4   *Minimizing Stress*

- Acknowledge risk
- Set limits
- Change the environment
- Reconsider values
- Exercise
- Develop support systems
- Seek counseling
- Have a sense of humor

emotional, psychological, and medical complexity and intensity of the work can be overwhelming. Government regulations, paperwork, malpractice, negotiations with third-party payers, and regulatory agencies are major stressors for many clinicians, and the ethics consultant may have to face these as well.

One of the first steps in minimizing the personal stress of ethics consultation is to be aware of the problem. If the problem is severe, professional help may be needed. Table 3–4 lists some broadly applicable ways of minimizing personal stress and burnout.

Several authors have recommended at least nine practical solutions to burnout and impairment. Many of these solutions have not been formally tested, but seem sensible, and are listed as follows:

1. Acknowledge and identify the reversible and irreversible risk factors for burnout.
2. Incorporate healthful values for your practice, including respect for the patient as an individual, self-acceptance, recognition of personal vulnerability, effective limit setting, and acknowledgment of the natural course of events.
3. Change your environment, even for a short time. Vacations and weekends away are stress reducing. Calendar planning is essential; otherwise, hospital committee meetings may coincide with family vacations. Some specifics include:

   - Reviewing, with your family, the household calendar for six months, and putting these family dates in your pocket calendar.

- Reviewing, with your secretary, the projected committed events for the coming year, and putting these dates in your pocket calendar.
- Eliminating dual, unessential, and, when possible, unwanted commitments.
- Scheduling leisure time; it is as important as work time and deserves the same planning.
- Working at home one day each week, using a computer, modem, or fax machine.
- Maintaining one day each month without interruption or phone calls.

4. Reconsider or renew humanistic, spiritual, or aesthetic aspects of your life.
5. Exercise regularly. Physical activity serves as a mental relaxer and can overcome fatigue and increase the quality of sleep. It allows for time alone, a change of mental and physical pace, and an opportunity to unleash stress, in a socially acceptable manner.
6. Develop a social support system; such systems require time to develop and may come about through outside interests, such as sports, hobbies, or community groups.
7. Develop a medical support system; fellow physicians and nurses can listen, provide technical and emotional support, and hold colleagues accountable.
8. Seek professional counseling; even one or two sessions can be helpful in recovering perspective and bringing about positive changes.
9. Have a sense of humor. While ethics consultation is a very serious endeavor, the consultant should be able to laugh at himself or herself. Humor can reduce stress by humanizing a difficult situation.

CASE CLOSE

In the case of Mr. Gordon, the consultant was forced to adapt to a new health care system. The consultant had to adjust to the particular culture, mores, and political pressures of the

continued

nursing home. The nursing home was concerned about negative public relations if the daughter and physician agreed on tube feeding withdrawal. The legal counsel was concerned about losing a court battle against the daughter if the consultant decided that Mr. Gordon was not irreversibly ill and should be fed. Mr. Gordon was unable to speak, but his proxy, the daughter, had made her wishes clear. The question was whether Mr. Gordon's wishes would be the same as his daughter's if he could speak.

The emergency nature of the consultation, together with the urgency of the legal and clinical problems, directed the consultant to gather data expeditiously. The consultant found that Mr. Gordon did indeed seem to have an "incurable/irreversible condition" but thought that a neurologist should make sure that he did not have Parkinson's disease (a potential cause for his poor ability to swallow, his rigidity, and his mumbling). The consultant also recommended that if Mr. Gordon had Parkinson's, he should have an adequate trial of therapy. After speaking with his daughter, it was clear that Mr. Gordon had participated in similar decisions to discontinue life-sustaining treatment, not for himself, but for his wife years ago. Mr. Gordon's own values, as relayed by his daughter, doctor, and nurse, allowed leaving out the tube.

A neurologist did see the patient, and found that Sinemet was unlikely to help. Mr. Gordon died several days later. The legal counsel, on receiving a messengered copy of the consultation and several references with suggestions for institutional policy, said that the 17.5 hours that the consultant had invested had been "worth it" and decided not to pursue any further legal action against the family.

SUMMARY

Ethics consultants must earn credibility, which requires the demonstration of expertise and the ability to pay attention to the administrative vision and mission of the consultant's home institution.

The consultant must be affable, accurate, available, and affordable. Affable consultants listen carefully, pay attention to the needs and interests of others, and may be perceived as warm and caring. Accurate consultants note the details of diagnosis, prognosis, and treatment, as well as the details of the personal, social, familial, and financial aspects of a case. Reading and understanding published, thoughtful references can also improve the consultant's precision. Available consultants are accessible in person and by phone or beeper. Affordable consultants provide services at rates similar to those of other nonprocedure-oriented, cognitive specialists. Ethics consultation, while time-intensive, is much less expensive than most technological medical services.

Ethics consultants must write their own job description, because few institutions know what to expect. A formal job description clarifies the interests and objectives of both the consultant and the institution, and sets a standard for consultant performance evaluation.

Obtaining back-up coverage is a problem for many medical consultants, especially for solo or rural practitioners. As many as one in five consultations are urgent, if not emergent. Good back-up coverage will improve credibility and allow patients and clinicians easy access to assistance and expertise.

Institutions need vision and commitment to support the ethics consultant. Full-time consultants are best sponsored by a top manager in the health care institution. Effective sponsorship can give the consultant the resources necessary to do the job well. Sponsorship is also important if the consultant makes potentially unpopular recommendations, whether in a case or involving institutional policy.

Ethics consultants' compensation should be commensurate with their level of training and expertise. Ethics consultation, as a clinical service, can be paid for by patients and their insurance companies, including managed care organizations. Until reimbursement mechanisms are formally recognized, however, most consultants will continue to donate at least some of their time, energy, and expertise. Many consultations involve detailed medical histories, straightforward physical examinations, and highly complex decision making.

Obtaining hospital privileges requires consent from the medical staff. In academic medical centers, department chairs and deans who will act as sponsors can assist consultants in obtaining staff privileges.

Malpractice coverage is not specifically available for ethics consultants, but consultants may be covered as members of the hospital staff. Consultants should have malpractice insurance commensurate with other medical subspecialists (at least $1,000,000/$3,000,000) as a condition of employment. Usually, malpractice insurance is provided by the institution to all physicians who are its employees, and by a large medical group to its employees. Nonphysician ethicists applying for privileges should also obtain malpractice coverage through the medical staff office or a medical group. As part of malpractice prevention, the ethics consultant, like other consultants, should maintain good documentation to illustrate his or her reasoning process and actions taken in individual cases. Clear documentation can assist in the defense of a potential lawsuit.

The ethics consultant's skills can be evaluated, and the performance evaluation should depend on the job description. Consultants should keep up with relevant changes in medicine, law, and ethics. A computer data base, such as MEDLARS or COLLEAGUE, can be helpful in finding current information to help with cases. BIO-ETHICSLINE may be helpful for researching the philosophical and humanities literature. Major journals of professional societies and ethics centers, together with the print and nonprint lay media, currently provide accessible, timely assistance for keeping up.

Similarly, consultants should have access to and be familiar with the literature and opinions from each of the major specialty bodies in medicine. Relevant case law and statutory law, both state and federal, should be read in detail, as should copies of major legal opinions in health care law.

Ethics consultants work in a variety of institutions. Consultants in university teaching hospitals are faculty of the medical school with which the hospital is associated. They are actively involved in university-affiliated ethics centers and medical school ethics courses and often teach both in the classroom and on the wards. The ethics consultant's teaching role is also important in the community teaching hospital, but the nature of the teaching is different. Instead of the didactic teaching of ethics fellows, house officers, and medical students, with whom the consultant may play a secondary role, the consultant offers practical clinical analysis and advice to staff physicians, nurses, families, and patients. In the nonteaching hospital, the ethics consultant is primarily a practitioner, teaching as part of his or her daily work and by example. The ethics consultant must demonstrate credibility, however, before hoping to be consulted on especially tough cases. In for-profit settings, consultants can help foster moral accountability. Consultants in long-term care may be faced with patients who have estranged families or are isolated and vulnerable, without reliable surrogates. In nonteaching rural hospitals, access and confidentiality problems are predominant. Many small communities are unable to support a full-time ethics consultant, so the consultant will probably need to practice in his or her primary field more than his or her urban counterpart.

Like other areas of clinical care, ethics consultation is personally stressful, and ethics consultants can experience burnout. Symptoms of burnout include the avoidance of consultations, tardiness, absenteeism, poorly charted observations, and a search for relocation. Consultants may prevent or diminish burnout through attempting to incorporate sensible personal and professional priorities.

4
Consultants
and Committees

The consultant can present the case to the committee.

Ethics consultants and ethics committees are synergistic, complementary components of an institution's ethics program. Consultants and committees work together but generally have distinct tasks — for the consultant, clinical care and for the committee, policy matters. Although both consultants and committees are active in professional education, committees will usually take the lead in considering legal and economic dilemmas.

This chapter will explore the synergistic relationship between consultant and committee, using patient care examples to describe ways in which consultants and committees have worked well together. The consultant and the committee can use each other's strengths to benefit patients, families, staff, and institutions. In addition, the consultant should develop relationships with other institutional ethics committees, such as institutional review boards (IRBs), quality assurance (QA), peer-review organizations, utilization management, risk management committees, and impaired physician committees.

THE CONSULTANT/COMMITTEE RELATIONSHIP

If the chair of the committee is a trained consultant, then he or she can provide consultation in a skillful, timely fashion and use the strengths and resources of committee members for assistance. Often, the consultant is the chair or co-chair of the ethics committee and may go to see the patient, do the consultation, and report back to the committee at its regularly scheduled meeting. Or, the consultant chair may form a consulting subcommittee of several members, using their individual strengths at the patient's side or with other clinicians as other pairs of eyes and hands in performing the consultation. A subcommittee can have distinct political advantages when its members are from different areas of the hospital and are able to address the concerns of their own colleagues. Chapter 2 briefly outlines these approaches, but they will be considered in more detail here.

Many ethics committee members are interested in hearing about and even deciding issues of patient care, yet these members often lack training, expertise, and resources in clinical ethics. Without strong clinical leadership and support, ethics committees have little clinical credibility and cannot offer strong educational efforts. As a result, members of these committees are unable to expand their knowledge of clinical ethics.

How then do ethics committee members participate in patient care issues?

The answer to this question is found in the actions of the most effective consulting committees. Invariably, these committees have one or more members who are developing the skills and beginning to perform the roles of ethics consultants. Many ethics committee chairs function as ethics consultants in hospitals, long-term care facilities, managed care organizations, and ambulatory care centers. Ethics committee chairs who function as ethics consultants talk with requesters, see patients, review charts, gather data, and offer advice. Ethics committee chairs who are acquiring the skills and performing the roles of clinical ethicists are learning to be ethics consultants.

Consultants who are not committee chairs can also inform the committee about their consultations and assist the committee in several ways. Committee members can learn the consultant's approach to the patient, including which facts they need to understand and analyze to help resolve different cases. Some committee members may wish to pursue further training in ethics, through, for example, a postgraduate fellowship or an advanced degree in health care ethics. Committees may also be able to provide the consultant with a constructive, collegial, multidisciplinary critique of his or her work in a case.

In turn, ethics committee members can promote the consultant's availability to colleagues and can offer emotional and political support to the consultant, who will often find cases draining and difficult. As an administrative ear, ethics committees can provide a needed sounding board for the consultant.

In general, ethics committees function best in considering broader, institutional issues, such as advance directives and financial conflicts of interest. The consultant can help the ethics committee by providing actual cases as a springboard for discussion and by alerting committee members to the particular policy issues that they raise. This enables members to debate, develop, and implement patient-centered policies.

Ethics committees that lack a trained clinical ethicist should not consult on individual cases. Patients deserve the personal care offered by an ethics consultation service or ethics subcommittee led by a trained consultant. A patient-centered approach is more likely to achieve the goals of care than is an administrative deliberation. In general, ethics committees do not have the expertise to apply casuistic reasoning to a particular case or to advise requesting physicians on reasonable courses of action. It is difficult for large groups of committee members to work on individual patient cases. Whether their deliberations are open or closed, verbal or written, or optional or mandatory, and whether their consensus is a product or a process, most committees will not have properly seen the patient or gathered the appropriate information from those who are part of the team. In addition, most large committees lack clinical credibility and fail to document their findings adequately or to follow up on cases.

Ethics committees should not hold themselves out as decision-making bodies. If ethics committees become purely administrative or function as juries, physicians will abdicate their judgment to these (perceived) powers of law and regulation. More importantly, the personal element of ethics consultation will be lost. Ethics committees will then devolve into mandatory, regulatory boards, handing down rulings in major patient cases. This is a bad outcome for the patient.

Case Example: Entire Committee

Is there any role for the ethics committee in case consultation? It is possible for a united, experienced committee to support the patient and family. In this role, the committee can act as a sensitive, sympathetic board of concerned, interested people. The committee members must simply listen.

For example, Jennifer Sienas, a 25-year-old woman severely neurologically injured in a car accident, had been on the ventilator for several weeks and needed a tracheostomy to prevent tracheal stenosis. Her parents, deeply religious individuals, refused permission for the procedure. They worried that if they consented, Jennifer would have to be treated with all available therapy.

The ethics consultant reviewed the record, examined the patient, and spoke with the health care team and Jennifer's parents. The consultant recommended the tracheostomy to prevent permanent tracheal stenosis, which would be very uncomfortable for Ms. Sienas if she survived. The consultant noted, however, that all further decisions regarding treatment should be individually negotiated with the family and that medical treatments could be withdrawn if neurologic improvement did not occur.

After repeated attempts, the attending physicians and ethics consultant were unable to persuade the parents of this view. Acknowledging the impasse with the parents, the ethics consultant asked them to come to a meeting where a hospital chaplain would be present. The goal was to provide a supportive, nonjudgmental atmosphere for Ms. Sienas's parents to express their views. The consultant assured them that the committee could not "decide" their daughter's case.

At the ethics committee presentation, before Ms. Sienas's parents entered the room, the consultant presented the case to the committee. Ms. Sienas's parents were then invited into the room. They were introduced to the committee members, and they spent an hour expressing their concerns. The committee listened quietly, with the consultant asking questions of the parents from time to time. Several ethics committee members spoke near the end of the parents' visit, but the hospital chaplain, who shared the parents' faith, was quite direct. He pointed out that even if they accepted the tracheostomy, overall, Jennifer "was in God's hands." Her parents became silent as they considered these words, which were especially meaningful for them. They agreed to consent to the tracheostomy, and expressed gratitude to the committee and

continued

especially to the chaplain, who had addressed their refusal of
treatment on a spiritual level.

THE ETHICS SUBCOMMITTEE

The ethics consultant can also work with a subset of the ethics
committee. One such helpful subcommittee may include a health care
attorney, a nurse, a physician, and the consultant. In the best of
circumstances, all members see the patient, and, together, make an
assessment and suggest a plan that is broad, imaginative, and thoughtful.

All members of the subcommittee should be prepared to see the
patient. Members should have a plan for gathering information,
determining what information is missing, and regrouping to discuss
their assessments. Any member of the subcommittee who has not
seen the patient should be reluctant to offer advice on the case to the
requesting physician or team members. If no other subcommittee
members are prepared to see the patient, the consultant should
remain responsible for seeing and evaluating the patient and performing the consultation.

Consulting subcommittees may offer the consultant special advantages. When the requesting physician's request for help requires
unusual reassurance or psychological support, an empathic nurse,
psychologist, or social worker can contribute to the case management. While the consultant can usually supply both reassurance and
advice, the presence of an experienced colleague with a specialized
rapport or skill can provide, in some cases, the needed encouragement for the patient and the requesting physician.

Case Example: Consulting Subcommittee

A well-publicized Minnesota case[1] makes clear several points about
the complementary nature of trained consultants and consulting
subcommittees.

An 87-year-old woman with chronic obstructive pulmonary disease
fell down a flight of stairs and suffered a severe intracranial
hemorrhage. After several months of hospitalization, a persistent

vegetative state (PVS) was diagnosed and she was transferred to a long-term care facility. Approximately a year later, she developed sepsis and was transferred back to the acute care facility, where her respiratory status worsened and she required intubation and mechanical ventilation.

After two months, the ethics committee chair received a request for consultation from the attending physician who asked, "Is mechanical ventilation ethically required here? Is medical futility sufficient grounds to discontinue the ventilator, in the absence of known patient preferences?" The chair asked a consulting subcommittee, comprised of an ethics consultant (a general internist with ten years of experience in ethics consultation), a clergy member, and a nurse to see the patient.

The consultant reviewed the medical record, examined the patient, and spoke with her husband, her attorney, and the physicians, physicians-in-training, nurses, and social workers caring for the patient. He verified the absence of personal advance directives with the patient's husband and discussed and confirmed the diagnosis of persistent vegetative state with a consulting neurologist. The husband opposed discontinuing the ventilator, hoping for a miracle. The consultant asked the ethics committee nurse to talk with the team nurses. The ethics committee nurse discovered that the floor nurses had conflicting feelings about the patient's daily care. Many believed they were caring for a corpse, while others felt that the husband's deeply felt love for his wife made it reasonable to administer nursing care to her. The pastor pointed out the spiritual issues in the case and considered the issue of miracles with the consultant.

In the assessment, the consultant found that it was ethically permissible to discontinue the mechanical ventilator, as it no longer met any definable personal medical interests that the patient might have had. Along with the nurse, the consultant spent hours listening to and counseling the floor nurses caring for the patient; they also included the pastor in these discussions.

After the patient had been in the hospital for three months, the case received local media attention, and the

continued

patient's husband recalled his wife's specific directive to live as long as she could, even in PVS on a ventilator. The requesting physician resigned from the case because she was about to have a baby, and the patient's husband asked the ethics consultant (in whom the husband had developed great trust) to manage the case. The consultant did so, even while openly petitioning a local probate court for appointment of a neutral third party, instead of the husband, to be the patient's guardian. However, a local probate judge approved the husband's petition, over the objection of the attending physicians and the ethics consultant. The patient died three days later.

When participating directly in a patient's case, all members of the consulting subcommittee need an appreciation for the details of the case. In this case, the consultant could advocate for the patient's interests, attempt to assuage the patient's husband, and promote the health care team's decision-making and ethical framework, drawing on the skills and sensitivities of the other members of the subcommittee.

THE ETHICS COMMITTEE'S ROLE IN PROFESSIONAL EDUCATION

The educational role of the ethics committee can be broader than the case-centered educational role of the consultant. With its command of hospital policies and its access to institutional resources and community liaisons, the ethics committee can foster a discussion of issues that hospital employees and the community at large may find relevant. Didactic ethics seminars, grand rounds, continuing educational programs, and public lectures may be organized by the committee as a regular part of a hospital's educational effort for its staff.

The ethics committee can assume a leadership role in the design and dissemination of a basic core curriculum for institutional staff faced with clinical ethical problems. Before attempting to capture an institution-wide audience, the committee should start with self-education and work through a structured, rigorous curriculum. Although it is ambitious to design an institution-wide curriculum in clinical ethics, and even though the institutional staff will not be interested in each topic, the committee can serve as a thoughtful resource for those who are interested, while attempting to pique the interest of the staff as a whole.

Different institutions will focus on different areas, and each institution should have its own curriculum of general topics. For acute care institutions, topics may include DNR orders, living wills, brain death, the withdrawal of life-sustaining treatment, euthanasia, and abortion. For medical and nursing staffs, profession-specific topics are important and may include the doctor–patient relationship and dual loyalties for medicine, nurse–patient and nurse–physician relationships, and professional autonomy for nursing. Medical specialists may want to learn about topics that pertain specially to them; for example, the disclosure of HIV status to patients for surgeons, commitment and competency evaluations for psychiatrists, and maternal–fetal conflicts for obstetricians. Long-term care facilities may wish to undertake special seminars on "Do Not Hospitalize" (DNH) orders. Large health systems, medical groups, and clinics may be especially interested in the ethics of managed care and outpatient clinical ethics.

Table 4–1 outlines a sample general core curriculum for ethics committees wishing to teach hospital staff about ethical dilemmas in the acute care hospital. A more detailed, setting-specific curriculum, specifically tailored to the outpatient setting, follows it. Both curricula can be implemented using a lecture format, small group discussion, or individualized readings. Again, a single curriculum will not meet the needs of all hospital staff, but outlining the fundamentals is a beginning.

LEARNING CLINICAL ETHICS FROM CASES

Cases may raise both general and specific educational issues and serve to illustrate ethical principles. Some cases may also demonstrate paradigmatic, typical, or recurrent patient or staff needs and encourage staff to learn more about the issues raised.

Table 4–1   *An Ethics Committee Core Curriculum*

General Topics

I. Problems of patients
- A. Finding information
- B. Trusting and seeking an advocate
- C. Needing reassurance and encouragement
- D. Understanding and overcoming the financial barriers to receiving care
- E. Gaining a sense of control
- F. Wanting to prolong life
- G. Controlling chronic disease
- H. Improving quality of life
- I. Processing informed consent
- J. Understanding and using advance directives well
- K. Ameliorating symptoms, especially pain and dyspnea
- L. Addressing and resolving maternal–fetal conflicts
- M. Considering suicide and obtaining help
- N. Integrating spirituality in medical decisions

II. Problems of health professionals
- A. Enhancing clinician–patient communication
- B. Enhancing clinician–clinician communication
- C. Promoting professionalism and codes of ethics
- D. Developing and implementing clinical judgment
- E. Determining decision-making capacity
- F. Understanding surrogate decision making
- G. Withdrawing life-sustaining treatment
- H. Writing "Do Not Resuscitate" orders
- I. Using high-technology treatment
- J. Understanding the legal aspects of care
- K. Understanding and integrating the financial aspects of providing care
- L. Recognizing impairment and preventing suicide
- M. Increasing the regulation of clinical practice
- N. Balancing patient desires vs. clinical possibilities
- O. Forming personal value systems
- P. Discussing assisted suicide and euthanasia
- Q. Understanding the difference between withdrawing and withholding treatment

Table 4–1, Continued

Specific Topics for Office Practice

I. Problems of dual loyalty

   A. Financial conflicts of interest

   B. Malpractice prevention

   C. Referral to consultants

   D. Employers and employees

   E. Personal familial obligations

   F. Managed care tensions

II. Problems of autonomy and communication

   A. Psychological factors that influence decision-making

   B. "Difficult" patients

   C. Noncompliance

   D. Refusal of office treatment

   E. Lifestyle interventions

   F. Nonallopathic practitioners and alternative care

   G. Advance directives for health care

   H. Literacy and contracts

   I. Patient/family demands for "futile treatment"

III. Problems of professional and social responsibility

   A. Health activism

   B. Ambulatory education

   C. Pharmaceutical representatives

   D. For-profit care and research

   E. Community and the public health

   F. Compliance with state-mandated regulation

   G. Nontherapeutic use of authority

Case Example: Teaching Clinical Ethics Hospital-Wide

The issues of the quality of life considerations and the indications for a "DNR" order were raised by the following case.

> Mr. Burns, a 78-year-old man dying of metastatic lung cancer, was obtunded and unable to communicate. He was receiving treatment for pneumonia in the intensive care unit. His

continued

physician had asked him before he became unable to make decisions if he would want to be revived should he have a cardio-respiratory arrest. Much to the physician's surprise, Mr. Burns had insisted that he wanted to receive cardiopulmonary resuscitation (CPR) and could not be dissuaded from this position.

The ethics consultant saw and examined Mr. Burns and talked with his family about the medical procedure of CPR and its useful application in the event of a sudden, unexpected arrest. When asked about her father's reasons for apparently wanting CPR, Mr. Burns's daughter replied, "I'm not sure exactly why Dad wants it, but what's the harm in trying?" After speaking further with Mr. Burns's family, the attending physician convinced them that it was not likely resuscitation would work or be of benefit. A "Do Not Resuscitate" order was written. Several weeks later, Mr. Burns suffered a cardiac arrest and died without an attempt at resuscitation.

But the case had already provoked a heated debate among the nurses and physicians on the hematology–oncology floor and in the ICU. What about the other patients on the floor who had not been asked about resuscitation? Would attempting to resuscitate Mr. Burns have demonstrated respect for his autonomy, or would it have been a futile, even cruel exercise of medical technology? What would his quality of life have been if resuscitation had been successful? When is it appropriate for surrogate decision-makers and physicians to override the patient's prior stated wishes, especially without the chance to inform him? What should the nurse's role be in cases like Mr Burns's — patient advocate or family friend?

After the consultation, the consultant presented the case to the ethics committee. The consultant suggested a committee-sponsored, hospital-wide educational conference on the issues of CPR, medical futility, and patient preferences, using Mr. Burns's case as the basis for discussion. An interdisciplinary sample of the committee, including a physician, nurse, attorney, psychologist, and pastor, constituted the conference planning committee. The conference was widely publicized, and continuing medical and nursing education credits were made available to attendees. Department chairs were asked to send their house staff, and the conference was scheduled as the grand rounds of two departments. Over 200 health professionals from the institution attended, and the hospital's Media Services Department videotaped the proceedings for those who wished to review them.

THE ETHICS COMMITTEE'S ROLE IN COMMUNITY EDUCATION

Ethics committees should pay special attention to the needs of the community. The public is increasingly interested in ethical and legal issues involving health care. Statewide ethics education programs, such as Oregon Health Decisions, have culminated in accepted programs from state legislatures about allocation priorities.

To further community education and knowledge, ethics committees will need to assess the specific needs of the community. Once these needs are ascertained, ethics committees can organize public forums, beginning with popular subjects, such as informed consent and advance directives. Information can be disseminated to the community about the ethical aspects of patient care, such as confidentiality, and health care rationing. Videotapes of these sessions can be made available through the public library, cable access television, and retail stores.

Ethics committees can also play a role in procedure-specific patient education. If an institution specializes in performing certain procedures (for example, cardiac transplantation or hemodialysis), the consultant can work with committee members, including lay members, to produce procedure-specific educational materials to enhance patient participation in decision making. Consultants can also work with committees in this educational role. The consultant could invite one or two patients (for example, an articulate patient who has received a bone marrow transplant or one who has survived emergency CPR) to speak about their medical experiences. This would add the personal perspective missing from many medical educational conferences and would enliven the discussion of organ transplantation or CPR.

HEALTH FACILITY POLICY FORMATION

The purpose of policies is to use principles to persuade. Policies have the effect of law within health care institutions and are often based on federal, state, or case guidance. Policies help practitioners work within the law; when policies are constructed knowledgeably and implemented thoroughly, they can serve as blueprints for the development of educational programs.

Ethics committees have already begun to work effectively in response to administrative and legal requirements. Many committees have assisted institutions in preparing advance directive patient materials and in formulating hospital policies to meet the requirements of the Patient Self-Determination Act of 1990. It is anticipated that committees will assist institutions in responding to the implications of the Human Genome Project. Committees also regularly participate in policies that include the care of the medically indigent, the treatment of Jehovah's Witnesses, the withdrawal of life-sustaining treatment, and organ procurement from brain-dead patients.

Official institutional documents should be constructed through a consensus process sensitive to legal and political guidelines; multidisciplinary input allows the drafting of institutional statements that reflect a diverse, pluralistic view. Ethics committees can provide the setting for open, democratic, administrative processes of debate. Two case examples follow.

Case Example: Forming Health Policy

Gabrielle Hanson was a 22-year-old RN on the general medical ward of a large hospital. She was starting an intravenous line in an HIV-positive patient when she stuck herself deeply in the hand with the needle. She went to the employee health physician and was told that the needlestick represented a significant blood exposure. The physician suggested prophylactic AZT, and Ms. Hanson learned that she would have to pay for the six-week course of this medicine. She also learned that the hospital had no formal mechanism for counseling or treating employees who had sustained an

HIV-positive needlestick injury. She paid for and began taking AZT but asked her supervisors to find out whether the medicine could be provided without charge.

She informed the ethics consultant of her case. The consultant spoke with a hospital administrator, who noted the lack of a standing policy, the hospital's obligation to protect its staff, and the high cost of AZT to the nurse. The consultant presented the case to the ethics committee and suggested that it be used as a springboard for addressing the hospital-wide issue of HIV-positive needlestick injuries. The hospital administrator was present and pointed out that Ms. Hanson had already been promised reimbursement for her AZT. The administrator asked the committee to propose a policy that would define a significant needlestick injury, delineate the standard of care in treating such injuries, and provide for appropriate medical follow-up and psychological support for injured employees.

The full committee convened, and several hours of discussion ensued. The committee delegated the medical aspects of the policy to the hospital epidemiologist, the administrative and economic aspects to the vice president of the hospital, and the psychological support aspects to a clinical psychologist. Although Ms. Hanson had already received her treatment, counseling, and reimbursement for AZT by the time the committee convened, her case prompted a systemwide response to future injuries. The ethics committee did not need to respond quickly and resolve her case; rather, the committee used her case as a stimulus for moving toward a new employee health policy.

Implementation of a National Policy Mandate

Congress enacted the Patient Self-Determination Act (PSDA) in October of 1990. The PSDA took effect on December 1, 1991, and required hospitals, nursing homes, and hospices to advise patients upon admission of their right to accept or refuse medical care and of their right to execute an advance directive. Managed care organizations and home health care agencies are also required to provide the same information to each of their members upon enrollment.

Provider organizations also (1) document whether patients have advance directives, (2) implement advance directive policies, and (3) educate their staffs and communities about advance directives. Compliance with the PSDA is a condition for Medicare and Medicaid reimbursement and is tied to institutional Medicare contracts.

Ethics consultants and committees have acted as key institutional advisors to administration about the clinical care, policy, and education required by this act. Institutions with ethics programs were poised to comply with the PSDA, but some institutions lacking such resources scrambled for advice and counsel on how to comply. Policy formulation requires plans for implementation, and some ethics consultants and committees have taken innovative approaches to planning. These approaches include recording audiocassette tapes for staff, training primary care nurses to ask about written directives, producing videotapes for in-hospital television channels, and ensuring the separation of advance directives from quality assurance, utilization review, and risk management.

OTHER ETHICS COMMITTEES

Ethics consultants should be valued members of other institutional ethics committees, not just the medical staff or hospital bioethics committee. While the term *ethics committee* most often denotes an institutional bioethics committee, the ethics consultant will interact with a wide range of "ethics committees" of varying membership and goals. These committees include institutional review boards, quality assurance committees, peer review organizations and committees, utilization management committees, risk management committees, and impaired physician committees. Each of these other ethics committees is regulatory in nature and often relies on rules and regulations to judge research protocols, physician practices, and patient cases.

Membership on these committees may seem time-consuming and unproductive. Many consultants are not familiar with the agendas of these committees or the content of their deliberations. However, to varying degrees, these committees consider matters of ethical import to patients, families, and clinicians. If ethics consultants can contribute to these discussions, they may be able to assist patients and colleagues.

As with the institutional bioethics committee, the consultant is available as a patient advocate and especially as an expert in understanding and resolving patient care dilemmas. A committee may be especially interested in the occasional circumstances in which the doctor and patient (or investigator and research subject or hospital financial office and potential patient) have different interests. Here, the consultant relies on clinical skills and training. The consultant is still a patient advocate first, even if seemingly threatened by powerful interest groups or experienced investigators.

Institutional Review Boards (IRBs)

Clinical research is the foundation of medical care, and ethics consultants often function in hospitals with research programs. As consultants struggle to define the needs of patients as subjects and doctors as researchers, they can anticipate conflicting obligations. In clinical research, ethical issues arise that involve disputes between patients, investigators, health care institutions, and entrepreneurs. The consultant's skills as mediator and negotiator will be valuable in this setting, but as an advisor to the IRB, the consultant's role of patient advocate should predominate.

The ethics consultant can help the IRB in learning to identify the salient ethical aspects of research protocols. Consultants have been able to assist institutional review board members in refusing unethical research protocols and in approving promising research protocols that might yield valuable new scientific information but were politically unpopular. The consultant can assist IRB members in at least six ways.

1. The consultant can examine each protocol with the IRB to help it distinguish between research and therapy. This distinction may be especially unclear in Phase IV or postmarketing clinical research or when an investigator seeks to evaluate a therapy or procedure that would ordinarily be billed.

2. The consultant can support the IRB's rigorous inquiry about the efficacy and safety of proposed research tools, including the value of scientific information to be discovered.

3. The consultant can ensure that the IRB carefully addresses the enrollment of especially vulnerable patients, including those with impaired decision-making capacity or those who may become unable to make health care decisions.

4. The consultant can safeguard the process of informed consent by ensuring that an investigator personally asks subjects if they wish to enroll, instead of simply providing them with a written form.

5. The consultant can help point out potential financial conflicts of interest that exist between the hospital, the physician/investigator, and the patient.

6. The consultant can make certain that access to expensive research protocols is defined by standard scientific criteria.

When the National Commission for the Protection of Human Subjects of Biomedical and Behavioral Research defined research as a class of activities designed to develop or contribute to generalizable knowledge, the Commission was referring to clinical research involving human subjects. Being able to differentiate clearly between research and therapy is central to the ethics consultant's judgment. In advising the IRB, the consultant attempts to maintain a perspective that emphasizes the patient's good over the production of knowledge. If the research methods may deceive or injure a patient, the consultant helps the IRB to balance the project's technical validity with notions of respect for person and social justice. Knowing, for example, that cancer patients near the end of life are unlikely to be reasonably autonomous is part of a consultant's expertise. These patients find it especially difficult to make objective choices, and they rely on their physicians to help them.

IRBs are a regulatory ethics committee and may be the model for institutional ethics committees. IRBs must comply with rules and regulations concerning clinical research in response to a presidential mandate (resulting from the 1970s work of the Commission)[2] and to federal legislative and departmental instruction. Institutions must have policies concerning fraud and abuse to receive any federal funds for research. IRBs and the institutional official must review protocols for all research performed in the institution. IRBs have considerable clout and recognition; for example, at the end of the methods section of most peer-reviewed scientific medical papers is an acknowledgment of the IRB's approval of the papers' protocols.

Quality Assurance (QA)

Quality assurance (QA) is motivated by the organizational charge to maintain an acceptable standard of care. Quality assurance is designed to perform surveillance and corrective actions and to ensure that physicians practice within current norms, increasingly outlined by medical and regulatory organizations as practice parameters. QA hopes to teach physicians about these parameters and improve patient satisfaction, which is consistently linked to the personalness of care. QA committees restrict patient care to services that are necessary. The definitions of *necessary*, *appropriate*, *basic*, and *essential* have significant financial and ethical implications.

Ethics consultants assist QA committees confronted by moral dilemmas in their work. The consultant can help evaluate quality indicators, describe clinical areas of ethical interest, and provide feedback. The consultant may be asked by the chair to prepare remarks on subjects the committee is concerned about; for example, proper documentation of the reasons for a DNR order or the institutional use of specific consent forms.

Ethics consultants should not provide specific QA feedback to individuals. Providing this feedback is a circumscribed legal duty that rightly belongs to those actually involved in the review process. Should the QA committee have concerns about the behavior of specific physicians, and appeal these concerns to the consultant, the consultant should direct the committee toward established channels of physician discipline, such as department chairs, medical staff presidents, or, when appropriate, credentials committees or impaired physician committees.

Policies with ethical implications must be clinically monitored, and compliance with these policies should be evaluated. In most institutions, QA activities are coordinated by an on-site individual who works with the ethics consultant and the ethics committee to develop specific areas of clinical and ethical scrutiny. In long-term care institutions, common ethical problems can be identified for QA monitoring, with appropriate indicators for evaluation (see Table 4–2). These problems include decisions to withhold or withdraw life-prolonging treatment, the use of artificial nutrition and hydration, and the application of chemical and physical restraints.

Quality assurance review has revealed some important problems with appropriate care and with ethical practice in long-term care institutions. In one case, a family forced an incompetent patient to sign a living will; in another, a patient on enteral tube feeding was unable to absorb the food from the GI tract. In other cases, physicians did not co-sign DNR orders, or they wrote that a patient was terminally ill when a proxy produced a written advance directive from the patient. The QA chair could ask the ethics consultant how to evaluate each of these cases and how to publicize and promulgate proper standards of practice.

The ethics consultant might respond by stressing the need to avoid the role of a "moral police officer." On the other hand, the consultant might agree that an ethics consultation could have assisted in some of these cases. The consultant could suggest that the

Table 4–2   *Sample QA Assessment of Withholding/Withdrawing Decisions*

1. **Informed consent**
   - Consent from appropriate decision maker
   - Consent documented
2. **Clinical appropriateness of advance directive**
   - Living will
   - DPA
   - DNR authorization
3. **Terminal illness/irreversible unconsciousness**
   - Physician certification
4. **Appropriate use of forms**
   - Current dating/updating
   - No telephone authorization acceptable
   - Forms filled out completely and appropriately

QA chair contact the ethics committee chair to formulate a plan to educate physicians about limited treatment plans. The QA committee could promote and encourage nonpunitive, educational efforts with copies of empiric studies that would accompany any recommendations made about its subjects of review. The consultant could suggest that future QA activities focus on whether the educational interventions have improved actual compliance with policies.

Some hospitals have established a committee hierarchy that allows quality assurance committees to report their general concern about trends of physician action and practice to institutional bioethics committees. For example, if the QA chair has seen several cases of poorly documented advance directives, the QA committee may ask: "Nurses are discovering advance directives, but physicians are not recognizing, understanding, or following some advance directives. Is this a policy implementation problem or a guideline problem?" In this way, QA committees can bring matters of ethical concern to an administrative forum that has the authority and expertise to approach them. In general, this is far superior to appealing administrative difficulties to the consultant, unless the consultant also chairs the institutional ethics committee.

Continuous Quality Improvement (CQI)   Continuous quality improvement and quality assurance are related concepts. Many health care organizations and professional associations have adopted CQI as a key strategy for implementing their missions over the next decade. CQI is an ongoing effort to improve performance by monitoring and evaluating empirical data about key processes and outcomes. Many businesses outside of health care have embraced CQI as a way of enhancing performance, decreasing errors, and improving morale. Although the method is new and untested in health care, the consultant can act as a member of the CQI team as it develops checks and balances, and as it attempts to improve processes and outcomes. CQI itself has major ethical assumptions as it strives to be empirically based and is customer-satisfaction driven. The former assumption is clinical; the latter is usually financial.

Peer-Review Organizations (PROs) and Committees

Peer-review is defined by the JCAHO as "effective mechanisms to monitor and evaluate the quality and appropriateness of patient care and the clinical performance of all individuals with delineated clinical privileges. Important problems in patient care are identified and resolved, and opportunities to improve care are addressed. . . . "[3] Peer-review is less focused on resource use than is utilization review, but both peer-review organizations and utilization review committees have mechanisms to evaluate the appropriateness of care.

Peer-review organizations can play a key role in setting local quality of care standards. Using consensus panels of experts and subcommittees of their membership, PROs establish quality indicators and review charts retrospectively (as do many QA committees) to determine which have fallen outside the local standard of care. Informal and local standards now exist for documenting informed consent procedures, writing DNR orders, and evaluating and implementing written advance directives. Should chart review reveal a wide variance from the standard of care, the ethics consultant may be asked to evaluate the record and give an expert opinion on the ethical permissibility of the physician's action in the case.

Ethics consultants can be members of and advisors to peer-review organizations that wish to articulate local standards of care. It is important for patients and physicians not to conflate the administrative and legal roles of the PRO with the clinical and educational roles of the consultant. The PRO, even more than QA, represents a quasi-legal body. Individual physicians who are subjected to a peer-review proceeding that might result in a loss of clinical privileges have the right to a hearing and to be represented by an attorney, to call and cross-examine witnesses, and to receive a written statement at the end of the hearing.

PRO committees need expert clinical, ethical, and legal advice. When the consultant can participate knowledgeably, he or she should do so. Peer-review represents a way of improving the standard of practice and assisting in patient advocacy.

Utilization Management (UM)

Utilization management assesses the medical necessity for care, the appropriateness of specific services and treatment modalities employed, and the cost of treatment. As previously noted, *necessity*, and *appropriateness* are key words that connote cost constraints in health care. In some hospitals, private utilization management firms are hired to provide prospective, concurrent, and retrospective case management. Some physicians who participate in these committees do so reluctantly, yet these committees offer an opportunity to influence individual patient cases and physicians, and have great authority in managed care organizations.

Although utilization management is designed to promote quality care, physicians view it differently. The American Medical Association has reported that 20 percent of over 4,000 physicians surveyed found utilization review to be the single factor that interferes most with clinical decision making; for internists, the figure was 30 percent. Preadmission or preprocedure certification and retrospective review were named as the most intrusive and most time-consuming.[4] In addition, practitioners have reported disagreements among reviewers about what should comprise appropriate care, uncertainty about reviewer qualifications, and disquiet about reviewer requests for confidential patient information. Utilization management attempts to assess the medical necessity and appropriateness of diagnostic and therapeutic modalities and to ensure that patients do not receive unnecessary services.

The ethics consultant's relationship to utilization management is different from the QA and peer-review organization relationships. Generally, the consultant should avoid active membership on the committee but may act in an advisory capacity. As usual, the consultant's role is educational and patient centered. Again, neither ethics consultants nor ethics committees should provide specific utilization or peer-review feedback to individuals; this is a circumscribed legal duty that rightly belongs to those actually involved in the review process.

Like QA committees, utilization committees may encounter matters of ethical concern in their work. Similarly, utilization committees may wish to report their findings to ethics committees, which can then consider a general course of action if policy changes are needed. The consultant can encourage this reporting relationship, as ethics committees should be aware of the kinds of care that utilization review considers to be inappropriate and unnecessary. Institutional policy can help persuade providers to remain patient advocates in the face of utilization constraints, and ethics committees here can function as patient advocates.

Utilization committees may ask the ethics consultant about specific cases. In general, the consultant should avoid making judgments about the moral propriety of an individual case. For example, a primary physician is thought to have "gamed the system" by keeping an intravenous line in a hospitalized patient so that the patient could receive what the physician and patient judged to be needed hospital care for another day. However, utilization management does not believe the extra day was necessary. The consultant might assist utilization management and the physician by suggesting an open, separate, professional discussion of those circumstances under which actions like "gaming the system" may be clinically and ethically supportable. Many physicians do not realize that the economic constraints on such cases can be successfully appealed to UM first, and through the courts, if necessary. One California patient won her case after she was discharged because of utilization pressures.[5]

In some cases, consultants may make an assessment that care is necessary based on the patient's personal situation and medical condition, even when this assessment conflicts with the utilization review interests or the protocols of practice parameters. Practice parameters are likely to be recognized by utilization review committees and, as a result, may dictate future practice in some areas; this can present ethical problems for patients and physicians. Although parameters for the diagnosis and management of even common medical problems can be drawn from scientific data bases, such data bases are nearly always incomplete and may be inadequate. Parameters may become maxims instead of tools, and individual patient preferences and circumstances may then be overridden. Such parameters are symbolic of a movement from highly discretionary doctor–patient visits to more standardized and regulated encounters.

Risk Management

Risk management is a systematic approach to "making and carrying out decisions, tasks and activities that will prevent, reduce or minimize legal and financial losses to individuals (such as a medical staff) or an organization (such as a hospital)."[6] Risk management is linked conceptually to quality improvement; its processes of risk identification, measurement, and treatment (with risk control and risk financing) are its basic elements. Institutional risk managers review all incident reports filed. They conduct educational programs, offer advice on health care policy, and encounter ethical dilemmas as they seek compliance from hospital staff members through regulations.

An effective risk manager can be an important ally of the ethics consultant. Risk managers and ethics consultants can work together, especially when the issue of withdrawal or withholding of life-sustaining treatment arises. Financial, legal, and publicity risks to a health care institution in end-of-life decisions are minimal, compared with routine medical and surgical care. Even if the ethics consultant sees the most difficult cases, few such cases will end up in court because of patient or family dissatisfaction.

Risk managers may tend to act more conservatively than most practitioners. For example, they are sometimes even more concerned than physicians about the implications of the withdrawal of treatment. In fact, it is more likely that institutions and individuals will be sued for providing unwanted treatment than for withdrawing unwanted treatment. Kapp has written that "a more realistic and pragmatic assessment of risk should suggest greater deference to patient and family values regarding the aggressiveness of medical treatment near the end of life."[7] The same arguments about aggressive medical treatment hold for commonly used but burdensome treatments. For example, the ordinary application of mechanical restraints can, and sometimes does, result in patient injury. Many suits have been filed because of injuries resulting from restraints applied for indications of convenience or control. Here, the ethics consultant who advises untying the mitted hands of a 60-year-old patient with postoperative respiratory failure can rely on his or her knowledge of effective risk management and persuade the risk management committee about the humanity and overall safety of this gesture.

Ethics consultants should encourage risk managers to have a broad, pragmatic view of costs — personal, ethical, and public relations costs should be considered. Occasionally, consultants and risk managers disagree about such costs. For example, a risk manager may be concerned about a restrictive state law on the withdrawal of tube feeding when the consultant advises that tube feeding be withheld from a severely demented, terminally ill 84-year-old patient whose family strongly refuses the tube. The consultant should encourage the risk manager to identify the conflict between the hypothetical financial loss and the ethical obligation to honor the family's wishes. The consultant may be able to negotiate with the risk manager to find an ethical approach to the treatment plan.

Impaired Physician Committees

In the past two decades, important demographic research on impaired health professionals has emerged: most are rural family physicians in solo practice who abuse alcohol. A growing number are hospital-based anesthesiologists who abuse narcotics. A small minority of impaired physicians have an impairing psychiatric illness instead of, or in addition to, an addiction. Some hospitals and medical staffs have formed impaired physician or physician assistance committees to confront impaired physicians and help them into treatment.

Ethics consultants may be asked by such committees how to approach impaired physicians. The consultant may also be asked to assist in defining and characterizing impairment (for example, Is a physician with Pickwickian syndrome impaired?) and in developing hospital or medical staff policy that relates to substance abuse and drug testing (for example, the drug or HIV testing of employees, including physicians).

The ethics consultant attempts to assist the impaired physician committee, or if approached by the medical staff or administrative leadership, advises the formation of such a committee, led by an expert in substance abuse treatment. Responding to impairment is a professional responsibility, but it also may be an area with which the consultant is unfamiliar. Because a separate body of knowledge in the study and treatment of addiction has now arisen, and successful strategies have been employed to assist such patients, others may also have a special interest in assisting impaired physicians.

Key ethical questions that the consultant can raise for the committee to address include: When and how do physicians obtain treatment for impairment? Do physicians treat chemically dependent physicians differently than other chemically dependent people? Why is a different language used to describe physicians who abuse substances than is used to describe other chemically dependent people? Here, the consultant's duty is to be available to advise about the ethical issues in general, instead of deciding how or whether to approach a particular physician.

Physicians and nurses involved in ethics consultation may, like other health professionals, suffer impairment. As institutional workers, most nurses will be eligible for assistance from employee programs.

FUTURE TRENDS

In the years ahead, the ethics consultant can be expected to take on greater clinical responsibility. Major new trends in ethics consultation are emerging in the areas of clinical care, hospital administration, and consultation finances.

Clinical Care

The clinical acceptance of different models of ethics consultation is likely, if each can be shown to be educational and helpful in patient care, of high quality, and productive of good outcomes in cases. Many more clinicians will enter training programs, and the four key training programs noted in Chapter 2 may give rise to others. For now, the postgraduate fellowship programs will likely give rise to most of the academic leaders in the field, while the seasonal seminar programs may produce the most practitioners.

To establish the discipline in the clinical, scientific, and academic communities, research data using satisfaction, outcome, and quality measures will be essential. The success of clinical ethics training will depend on formal training programs that have prescribed standards, undergo rigorous evaluation, train a significant number of practitioners in well-defined practices, and improve patient care measurably. The success of training may also, in teaching institutions, depend on the graduates' ability to meet criteria for academic respectability (for example, through grants, publications, patient care revenues, and teaching).

Hospital Administration

Administrative trends presently include the careful delineation, approval, and evaluation of staff privileges in ethics consultation; requirements for established, accredited organizations to have ethics consultation mechanisms, especially when clinical disagreements arise; the state and federal regulation of ethics consultation services, especially as they pertain to life-sustaining treatment; and the growth of several new specialty societies in ethics, with the formal formation of an ethics board or governing organization to act as a political lobby and accrediting organization. These latter specialty societies may arise around a particular ethical issue (for example, life-sustaining treatment, health care rationing, or the new genetics), or they may arise as research bodies, as responses to regulation in medicine, or as advocates for appropriate compensation.

Consultation Finances

Financial trends in ethics consultation are directly related to both clinical and administrative trends. The financial future of consultation rests in its ability to earn credibility and distinction in its work and to meet standard criteria for distinction. Clinical research with peer-reviewed and published datasets will be critical in demonstrating ethics consultation's worth.

Discussions of financial trends also speak to the personal and cognitive nature of consultation services. Those who finance health care must recognize the cognitive, personal services that ethics consultants offer, that patients and families want, and that attending physicians request. Making consultation more available to clinicians who seek the services of an ethics consultant is part of appropriate recognition.

SUMMARY

Ethics consultants and ethics committees can and should work together. The consultant may often be the chair or co-chair of the ethics committee and may do the consultation and report to the committee at its regularly scheduled meeting. Alternatively, the consultant may form a consulting subcommittee of several members to bring particular insights to particular patient cases.

The most effective ethics committees have one or more members who possess the skills and perform the roles of an ethics consultant. Ethics committee chairs should prepare to function as ethics consultants in hospitals, long-term care facilities, prepaid health care organizations, ambulatory care centers, and in-home health care.

The ethics committee's educational role is broader than that of the consultant. Seminars, grand rounds, continuing educational programs, and public lectures may be organized by the committee. Each committee should undertake a core curriculum of general topics (DNR orders, living wills, brain death, the withdrawal of life-sustaining treatment, euthanasia), setting-specific topics (DNH orders in nursing homes, HMO ethics in the outpatient setting), profession-specific topics (the doctor–patient relationship and dual loyalties for medicine, nurse–patient and nurse–physician relationships, and professional autonomy for nursing), and specialty-specific topics (disclosure of HIV status to patients for surgeons, commitment and competency evaluations for psychiatrists, maternal–fetal conflicts for obstetricians).

Ethics consultants and committees have collaborated on policy issues, such as the Patient Self-Determination Act of 1990. As committee chairs or co-chairs, consultants educate and inform committees when it is appropriate to take on institution-wide initiatives.

Ethics consultants can act as members of and advisors to the IRB, and in this capacity, the consultant's patient advocacy role predominates. Consultants should also develop a good working relationship with the QA committee. For example, the consultant may be asked by the QA chair to discuss the documentation of DNR orders or compliance with informed consent forms.

Peer-review organizations (PROs) can play a key role in setting standards for the quality of care. Should chart review reveal a wide variance from these standards, the ethics consultant may be asked for an expert opinion. The ethics consultant's relationship to utilization review is different than the relationship to PROs and QA. Generally, the consultant should not be an active member of a utilization review committee but may act in an advisory capacity. The consultant's role should be educational and patient centered; the consultant is primarily an agent of the patient.

An effective risk manager can be an important ally of the ethics consultant. Even if the ethics consultant sees the most difficult or contentious patients and families, few such cases will end up in court.

Ethics consultants may be asked by impaired physician committees how to approach an impaired physician. They may also be asked to assist in cases of hospital employee impairment. Interventions in these cases are sensitive, but as a member of the institutional community, the consultant may play an intermediary, facilitative role by searching out those with greater authority and expertise to provide guidance.

Ethics consultants should have close relationships with IRBs, QA, PROs, utilization review committees, and impaired physician committees, but they should not mix the role of the consulting ethicist with the role of institutional manager or official. These other "ethics committees" have an explicitly regulatory nature. The consultant is not the institution's conscience but, ideally, should work to provide an ethical perspective for these committees, encouraging them to take this perspective as their own and valuing patient-centered goals. Ethics consultants should work with ethics committees and assist them in their work on institutional policy and education. This cooperation can result in long-term benefits for patients, physicians, and health care institutions. Future trends in consultation will include changes in training, with more trainees entering the field, and changes in staff privileges and remuneration.

Appendix
The Consultant at the Bedside: Illustrative Cases

The cases that follow are told as briefly, accurately, and faithfully as possible. The patients' names have been fictionalized. These cases attempt to show how a consultant acts in a case as it occurs. Most of the clinical particulars, moral reasoning, and ethical analyses are not recounted here. Almost all the quotations, however, were recorded at the time of consultation and speak clearly about the passion, intensity, and humanity of these stories.

The cases are grouped into six general categories:

1. Treatment refusals
2. CPR/DNR
3. Advance directives
4. Uncertain patient proxies
5. Decision-making capacity
6. Should we do more?

Neither the categories nor the cases are meant to be paradigmatic of a "case type" or an overarching rubric. Instead, the cases illustrate some of the difficulties that the consultant may expect to encounter when seeing patients. When deciding whether to present a few cases in great detail (the phenomenological tradition) or to present more cases in basic outline (the case presentation tradition), brevity prevailed. A detailed analysis of each case would have made this book overly long.

In some of these cases, the consultant made a mistake; these errors are noted because learning by others' mistakes can be useful.

In other cases, the consultant identified new ethical issues, addressing some, but not others; these are also noted, as it can be helpful to have another's sense of what seemed to work well and what did not. In some cases, the consultant appeared to solve the problem at hand.

In all cases, the consultant saw the patient, followed the patient at least until hospital discharge, and later asked requesting physicians how the consultation could have been more helpful.

Each case is presented in seven parts:

1. The question asked of the consultant by the attending physician ("Question")
2. The medical, social, familial, and personal aspects of the case ("Case")
3. The consultant's working and reasoning process toward an assessment and suggested plan ("Process")
4. The ethical options available to the requesting physician ("Options")
5. The physician's decision to accept or reject the consultant's assessment and suggestions ("Decision")
6. What happened to the patient ("Outcome")
7. A summary analysis of the consultant's actions in the case ("Summary").

The "Question" section represents the core elements of the case as the requesting physician understood them at the time. Although the question asked is not always about the key ethical issue in each case, it is important that the consultant address the requesting physician's question.

The "Case" section reveals the clinical details of each case as it evolved from past medical history to hospital admission and throughout the hospital course. Included in this section are those facts and circumstances that were apparent at the time of the consultation — part of the consultant's responsibility is to attempt to confirm the data presented.

The "Process" section shows how the consultant discovers and combines the details of the case, which often include medical data, patient preferences, quality of life factors, familial information, and economic facts. Articulating both the questions asked and other important, unasked questions is part of the consulting process.

The "Options" section contains the consultant's assessment and suggested plan and includes an attempt to provide direction in the case. In many cases, the consultant provides options for resolving other, newly identified ethical dilemmas and suggests new diagnostic tests or trials of therapy, a new financial or personal resource, or an innovative approach to a treatment plan. Recommendations for action are the most practical aspect of the consultant's written report; sometimes, the recommendations section is the only part that is read by the requesting physician.

The "Decision" section shows how physicians responded to the consultant's advice. Physicians may accept all, some, or none of the consultant's suggestions. In the majority of cases, there is no professional obligation for the consultant to insist that the suggestions be followed, nor is there a medical obligation for the requesting physician to follow the consultant's suggestions, although prudence may suggest otherwise.

The "Outcome" section shows that many patients survive to leave the hospital. Although the process of consultation is important, the consultant may want to reevaluate his or her methods and actions in a case if the final outcome is regrettable and could have been prevented.

The "Summary" section shows why the consultant acted as he or she did. Usually, the most important influences are not general ethical principles (for example, beneficence or autonomy), humanistic virtues (for example, respect or compassion), or regulatory dictates (for example, codes or laws). Instead, a principle, virtue, or law sometimes lends itself to the consultant's integration of the medical, social, and personal details of the case, which drive the consultant's actions. Contrasting cases are often pointed out in this section.

Many patients will accept physical examination, but refuse invasive treatment.

▎ *Treatment Refusals*

MARGARET REICHART

Question

"This patient refused a brain biopsy for a cerebral mass last month; but now that she lacks decisional capacity, her husband is insisting that we do a biopsy. Should we do it?"

Case

Margaret Reichart, 65 years old, was well until three months prior to admission when she noted a persistent, right-sided headache. Her internist ordered a computerized tomographic (CT) scan of the brain; the test showed a large right hemispheric mass suggestive of a primary neurologic malignancy. The consulting neurosurgeon proposed a biopsy with tumor debulking. Mrs. Reichart told the surgeon that she did not want any brain surgery. She did, however, agree to return to the neurosurgeon's office in two weeks to discuss surgery again. In another conversation ten days later, Mrs. Reichart again declined an operation, telling a neurosurgery resident, "God will take care of me; I am ready." However, Mr. Reichart said that he wanted his wife to have the biopsy.

Twelve days later, Mrs. Reichart was presented to the emergency department unable to speak and with left-sided hemiplegia. An emergency CT showed marked enlargement of the mass with intracerebral edema and shifting of the midline. Mr. Reichart requested a biopsy.

Process

The ethics consultant reviewed Mrs. Reichart's medical record and attempted to interview and examine her. He spoke with her primary physician, the consulting neurosurgeon and the resident, and Mr. Reichart and his two daughters. A hospital attorney advised the consultant of the husband's legal standing. The consultant concluded that Mrs. Reichart, when she had recently been able to participate in her own health care decision-making, had refused the proposed operation.

Options

The consultant's note stated that a biopsy would violate the patient's clearly expressed wishes and undermine the trust inherent in the physician–patient relationship. Moreover, performing the biopsy might no longer be indicated, as the rapid growth of the tumor made it unlikely to respond to surgery or chemotherapy. The consultant suggested that an empiric, palliative trial of radiotherapy might restore Mrs. Reichart's ability to participate in decision-making while still honoring her refusal of surgery. Finally, the consultant pointed out that because Mrs. Reichart had wished to be allowed to die without heroic intervention, cardiopulmonary resuscitation would not be consistent with her wishes. Continued documentation of conversations with the family, a "Do Not Resuscitate" (DNR) order, and a trial of radiotherapy were advised.

Decision

A radiotherapist was consulted, and a DNR order was considered. On the third hospital day, however, Mr. Reichart petitioned a probate court for guardianship. The ethics consultant and the hospital attorney considered contesting the guardianship but decided against it. A guardian *ad litem*, appointed to represent Mrs. Reichart's interests in the proceedings, advised the court of Mrs. Reichart's refusal of surgery. The judge granted Mr. Reichart legal guardianship of his incapacitated wife and empowered him to consent to biopsy. Mr. Reichart again requested that the neurosurgeon operate, who again refused. Mr. Reichart then found one of the surgeon's colleagues to perform the biopsy.

Outcome

The biopsy revealed anaplastic astrocytoma. Mrs. Reichart remained hospitalized and received cranial irradiation for the next six weeks. Her speech improved sufficiently to enable her to converse, although her hemiparesis remained unchanged. The ethics consultant spoke with her again about her wishes.

"Did you want an operation, Mrs. Reichart?"

"No. I told the doctor that."

"Your husband asked us to do the biopsy. Did you ever talk about it with him?

"There's no point in making more trouble. He and I have lived together for 44 years. He knows what I think."

"Would you have another operation if you needed it?"

"No. I didn't want one before."

"Will you tell your husband that?"

Mrs. Reichart looked away and started to cry. On hearing of this conversation, the neurosurgeon noted that the husband/guardian would not consent to a DNR order. On the tenth hospital week, Mrs. Reichart became febrile and hypotensive and was transferred to the intensive care unit, where she survived two cardiac arrests within 24 hours and died after a third attempt at cardiopulmonary resuscitation.

Summary

The consultant acted to discover the medical details of Mrs. Reichart's brain lesion, the personal details of her husband's misguided but pained protection of her, and the social details of their religious beliefs and family unity. Although patient autonomy seemed key, as Mrs. Reichart was about to receive a procedure she had specifically declined, she was neither self-determining nor self-sufficient. The consultant attempted to rely on compassion and kindness, realizing that technological medical approaches had little to offer, but this attempt and realization were insufficient. The consultant's negotiation skills were also not enough, despite going back into the medical record to discover the adequacy of the patient's informed refusal.

The consultant erred by inadequately defending Mrs. Reichart's refusal and by not contesting the husband's guardianship in court. Although the chances of success in court were small, the process long and Mrs. Reichart's disease fatal, it was worth trying, as it was the only avenue left. Such an appeal would have been grounded in direct knowledge of the patient's wishes and of the husband's misrepresentation and desperation.

This case shows the importance of patient advocacy, including legal advocacy if necessary, and can be contrasted with the case of Mrs. Bauer that follows.

ELSA BAUER

Question

"Is this acutely ill patient competent to refuse surgery?"

Case

Mrs. Elsa Bauer is a 91-year-old former professional author and civic leader. A widow with a son and a daughter-in-law, she lives in a nursing home. She was admitted to the hospital with an acute abdomen, disoriented and febrile. Thirty-six hours after admission, she was oriented but still had an acute abdomen, was also hypotensive, and had not been treated with analgesics. Her family physician and surgeon wanted to operate, but Mrs. Bauer refused.

Process

After reviewing the medical records, the consultant spoke directly with the patient, who was in the ICU. It was 10 P.M. Mrs. Bauer said, "I've had a full life. I've had many operations, and they've all turned out badly." Her first operation was a hysterectomy at age 28, and her last operation was five years ago for cataracts, in which she lost her remaining sight. The physical exam showed normal mental status and direct and rebound abdominal tenderness. The consultant noted that Mrs. Bauer spoke with both eyes closed. Blood pressure was 92/60. The consultant then discussed the case with the patient's son and daughter-in-law, eliciting support for her decision to refuse surgery. They were reluctant but had spoken with her themselves, and she had been consistent in her wishes to refuse surgery. Her son said, "She always does this . . . she always says she doesn't want it and then she takes it." The consultant pressed the surgeon for data about the likelihood of survival with gallbladder necrosis. It was approximately 40 percent.

Options

The options were to put Mrs. Bauer on a morphine drip and let her die, to temporize while continuing to attempt to persuade her, or to use her family to help override her refusal based on her past history of initial refusal then reluctant acceptance of procedures.

Decision

Instead of making a final decision that evening, the surgeon and primary care physician decided to revisit Mrs. Bauer and go over the issues again the next morning.

Outcome

The primary care physician came in at 6 A.M. to see Mrs. Bauer and persuaded her to have the operation. Several hours later, the attending surgeon obtained informed consent, took Mrs. Bauer to the operating room, and removed her gangrenous gallbladder. Five days later, when Mrs. Bauer was asked if her doctors had done the right thing, she said, "Of course they should have operated!" Mrs. Bauer left the hospital without complications. The consultant recommended that her family's visiting hours at the nursing home be increased, and they were.

Summary

The consultant acted quickly in this case to examine the patient, meet with the family, and talk with the physicians. This was clinically required, as Mrs. Bauer's condition was urgent. The consultant attempted to act to further Mrs. Bauer's goals and balance these goals against her frequent reversal of fortune and mind, and against her physician's wish to help her out of a nearly impossible surgical circumstance. The case was resolved by waiting, and by elucidating and repeating her wishes to her, and to her family. Her son and daughter-in-law did not want her to die, and time was on her and their side.

It is important to distinguish between Mrs. Reichart's and Mrs. Bauer's refusals. Mrs. Reichart's refusal was unequivocal; Mrs. Bauer's was not. Mrs. Reichart had a certainly terminal condition; Mrs. Bauer did not. In both cases, advocacy for the patient was key. Overriding a patient's refusal with persuasion, admittedly a continuum with coercion, is sometimes justified in consultation.

LELAND HOPKINS

Question

"This patient's mother, who is a nurse, doesn't want me to tell her mentally retarded 50-year-old son that he has bilateral renal cell carcinoma, or that he needs nephrectomies and dialysis to live. Should I tell him? If so, can he consent?"

Case

Leland Hopkins, a 50-year-old mildly mentally retarded man with tuberous sclerosis, was admitted to the hospital with malignant hypertension. The workup revealed a large renal mass and mildly impaired renal function, with a creatinine of nearly 2. The patient's mother, an LPN who had worked on a dialysis unit, insisted that her son not be told of the diagnostic findings. Mr. Hopkins was discharged, and the consultant was asked to see him in the office.

Process

After reviewing current data on the diagnosis and treatment of renal cell carcinoma, the consultant scheduled three office meetings with Mr. Hopkins and his mother. Mr. Hopkins knew there was "something wrong with my kidneys" and thought that was why he was having severe headaches. The consultant told him that he might have to have a kidney operation and be on dialysis, so that he could live longer. Mr. Hopkins described dialysis as he had seen it on a television show, but his mother interrupted and said, "Let's talk about this when we get home, Leland." On physical examination, Mr. Hopkins' blood pressure was 210/110. The consultant palpated a large, firm right submandibular lymph node.

The consultant spoke separately with the patient's mother. She feared that her son would become very upset if he knew that he might not be able to work in a woodworking shop, which he enjoyed greatly, and would become physically ill if he was told he needed an operation. She said, "I know — I'm his mother." She added that she thought dialysis was "miserable" for most patients.

Options

Because the consultant had palpated the node, he suggested asking an oncologist about a metastatic workup, before a decision to operate was made. He recommended a biopsy of the right submandibular node; rediscussion with mother and patient together if the workup proved negative; and legal guardianship, if necessary, to permit Mr. Hopkins, who seemed to evidence some understanding of the subject at hand, to live longer. These data were necessary before considering telling the patient and fracturing relationships between patient, parent, and physicians.

Decision

An excisional biopsy showed a pleomorphic adenoma of the salivary gland. A CT of the brain, a bone scan, and a CT of the abdomen showed no metastasis of the renal cancer.

Outcome

No surgery has been performed to date. The consultant has seen Mr. Hopkins over a period of three years, and each time, he has deferred decisions to his mother, asking her advice and asking her to make decisions. Nevertheless, the patient wants to live, his condition has not worsened, and he is gaining weight. He has also been able to continue working. His blood pressure is under better control.

Summary

Again, time was integral in the consultant's continued action in the case, and the consultant continued to counsel both Mr. Hopkins and his mother. The legal tool of guardianship was considered, but the patient's closeness to his mother outweighed its use.

In Mr. Hopkins's case, the consultant balanced respect for Mr. Hopkins, who seemed able to make decisions, with respect for his mother, who had been responsible for his well-being his entire life. Because she had evidenced such faithful caring, her moral authority was great. Thus, her word carried the case, especially when medical harm did not appear to arise as a result of following her plan.

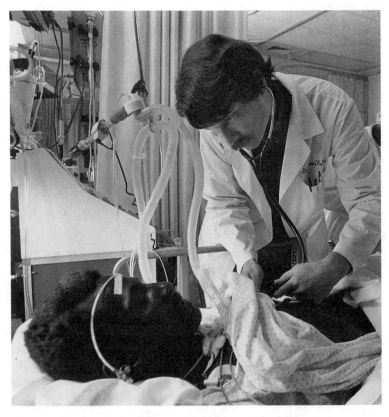

The consultant is often called to see the patient in the ICU.

CPR/DNR

SUSAN ABEL

Question

"Can I make the right decisions about treating my own mother-in-law who remains critically ill?"

Case

Mrs. Susan Abel is an 80-year-old with severe coronary disease who is ventilator and dialysis dependent and is stuporous. She entered the hospital two and a half months ago with unstable angina, had cardiac bypass surgery, and two weeks later developed an intestinal perforation. She had a laparotomy, but her obesity prevented primary closure of the incision. The patient's daughter is married to the attending physician. He has always taken care of Mrs. Abel; he has been her son-in-law and her doctor for 40 years. Mrs. Abel's husband insists on aggressive treatment, hoping that his wife will get better soon. Mrs. Abel's son-in-law requested the consultation himself, saying that other consultants had told him he should withdraw therapy and were uncertain whether he could be objective in the case.

Process

The consultant spoke with the attending physician briefly and informally, then reviewed the record, examined the patient, and spoke with the other consultants. The medication list did not reveal central nervous system depressants or analgesics. Mrs. Abel's electroencephalogram showed diffuse slowing. On physical examination, Mrs. Abel had a 12-by-10-centimeter subcutaneous abdominal defect with gross purulence. A neurologic exam showed unresponsiveness except to pain. A motor exam showed flaccidity in all extremities.

The consultant searched the medical literature for conflict of interest data, with particular attention to analyses of doctors who had treated their own family members. There were none, although the emotional complexity of playing the roles of both physician and family member was apparent. Data on the survival of critically ill patients revealed that Mrs. Abel's chances of surviving were less than 5 percent.

A large family meeting was held at the suggestion of the cardiologist with the consultant's acquiescence. Twenty people, including six physicians and several nurses, attended; Mrs. Abel's son-in-law ran the meeting. It lasted over an hour and ended with Mrs. Abel's husband and son-in-law agreeing to wait a while longer before making the decision to withdraw treatment. The consultant offered solace to Mrs. Abel's relatives and to the attending physician for his personal tragedy. The consultant met later and separately with the nurses, who voiced their affection for the attending physician but who were frustrated with caring for a patient who had been critically ill for so long with so little hope for survival.

Options

The consultant noted, "This is a critically ill elderly woman who is unable to make health care decisions and whose husband is directing aggressive treatment. In addition, Mrs. Abel's doctor is a close family member and is forced to be both attending physician and son-in-law. Fulfilling these two responsibilities seems impossible when caring for a critically ill patient."

The consultant strongly suggested that the attending physician transfer care of the patient to another physician. A second option would be to discontinue treatment. A third option would be to continue treatment and wait until Mrs. Abel either improved or died. The consultant also suggested a DNR order and a change in the goal of therapy from cure to palliation.

Decision

The cardiologist offered to take over the case, but the attending physician refused; he continued the patient's medicines but discontinued diagnostic and laboratory investigations.

Outcome

The cardiologist wrote a DNR order. Mrs. Abel died of a cardiac arrest two weeks after the consultation.

Summary

Here, the consultant gathered the medical details from the other consultants, as they had also managed much of the medical care. The social and personal details of the case came together quickly, as the attending physician and son-in-law were one and the same. The problem of physicians taking care of their own families is a surprisingly common phenomenon; many doctors think it causes trouble not only with judgment or objectivity, but with examinations and follow-up. Fairness to others and respect for others, including the nurses and physicians caring for Mrs. Abel, seemed the dominant principle here, and no codes or laws governed this practice. Although trained to meet Mrs. Abel's medical needs, the attending physician seemed too close to cope with bearing the bad news of a poor outcome of care. In addition, medical involvement with Mrs. Abel seemed to provoke and intensify intrafamily conflicts.

LORI NOLAN

Question

"Should this patient, for whom continued medical therapy is futile, be permitted her request for CPR, even though her family doesn't want her to have it?"

Case

Lori Nolan is a 27-year-old patient with a 20-year history of Friedreich's ataxia and a recent religious conversion to Christianity. Her disease has resulted in quadriplegia, deforming scoliosis, and a severe restrictive cardiomyopathy. Ms. Nolan put herself through college and obtained a degree in forestry. She recently moved several hundred miles to be closer to her boyfriend. She was admitted with gallstone pancreatitis and respiratory failure and was mechanically ventilated after a near respiratory arrest. At 5 A.M. on the fourth hospital day, her cardiologist wrote a DNR order "per family." However, when the ethics consultant saw the patient that morning, the order had been discontinued. Because the patient wanted CPR and her family disagreed, the cardiologist had asked the consultant to evaluate the appropriateness of CPR.

Process

The consultant read the record and saw the patient alone at first, and then with her boyfriend and father. Outside the room and with Ms. Nolan's father, her boyfriend described her attitude as "life, not death," and he noted that denial was a strong part of her coping mechanism. Ms. Nolan's father didn't want her to suffer anymore and had requested the DNR order. Privately to the consultant, her father also objected to her recent move to be closer to her boyfriend.

The consultant asked the cardiologist for the available data on survival after CPR. No specific numbers regarding Ms. Nolan's disease process were found, although data were available for patients who, like Ms. Nolan, had left ventricular ejection fractions of less than 20 percent. This data reported survival rates of less than 2 percent to leave the hospital. The cardiologist noted that Ms. Nolan had a tremendous will to live and might overcome apparently insurmountable odds.

On exam, Ms. Nolan was on the ventilator but able to nod and shake her head appropriately. She was in atrial fibrillation at a fast rate. She was quadriplegic and had anasarca. She nodded "yes" to the question, "Do you want CPR even if you have only a 2 percent chance of surviving?"

Options

The ethics consultant pointed out that Ms. Nolan had decision-making capacity and should be asked about medical decisions. The consultant also pointed out that the family members were not completely adversarial and would probably support Ms. Nolan's decision despite their differences of opinion. The consultant wrote, "It is easy to identify with this young, cheerful woman who is immobilized but fixes everyone with her smile." The consultant recommended that a heart transplant be considered, that Ms. Nolan's care be reevaluated after a reasonable period of time, and that significant efforts be made to incorporate the spiritual beliefs so important to her in her treatment plan.

Decision

Cardioversion of the atrial fibrillation was attempted, and the decision was made to resuscitate Ms. Nolan if she arrested.

Outcome

Ms. Nolan survived in the hospital for several more months and, despite several cardiac arrests, maintained consciousness and conversational ability before she suffered neurologic deterioration in the last several weeks and died.

Summary

This tragic case was marked by an intractable, terminal cardiac condition, Ms. Nolan's spirit and determination, and family members who could not agree on the goals of her care. Fortunately, Ms. Nolan was persistent in saying what she wanted, and the consultant tried to help her get it. Patient autonomy and physician beneficence were combined here, as the physicians believed doing good was getting her home. Respect for Ms. Nolan's personal beliefs, her courage, and the pathos of her condition made everyone fight just a little harder. Economic considerations were never explicitly raised for discussion, and even if they had been, the consultant would have lobbied for her expression of free will as authentic, deliberate, and heartfelt. In the analysis, advice, and advocacy, the ethics consultant factored in Ms. Nolan's choices, including a strong drive to live and a devout religious belief.

Although medical futility is a medical professional's judgment based on medical facts, such as efficacy, benefit, and safety, patients like Ms. Nolan are sometimes allowed to try to beat even a terminal illness. Will, determination, vigor, and medical uncertainty can combine to defy what many physicians, and some decision analysts, believe to be futile. Physicians may misdiagnose illness or overestimate futility, especially at the margin: these are unfortunate, inevitable mistakes for which patients should not have to pay. However, wanting a procedure that has a survival rate of less than 2 percent is a demand less acceptable to payers and physicians in the 1990s than it was in the 1980s. Future patients like Ms. Nolan may have fewer choices.

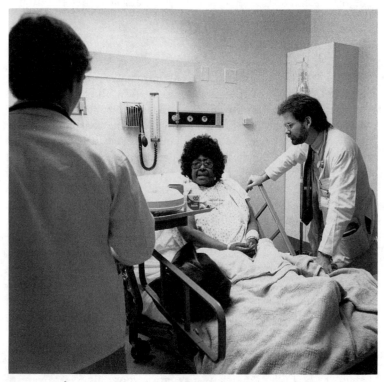

When asked, patients will usually tell the team what's important.

Advance Directives

JUDITH HUNTER

Question

"Is a living will appropriate for this postoperative patient with terminal cancer?"

Case

Judith Hunter is a 50-year-old woman with carcinoid of the bowel. Six months prior to admission, she underwent a right hemicolectomy with a presumptive diagnosis of appendicitis; the tumor was later diagnosed by pathology. Ms. Hunter has been hospitalized with recurrent bowel obstruction for six days. The day after admission, she underwent an exploratory laparotomy for symptoms of recurrent abdominal pain with nausea and vomiting; the operation revealed massive carcinomatosis. In addition, she had postoperative respiratory distress syndrome and necrotizing fasciitis of her abdominal wall. She had a wide excision for gangrene and myonecrosis two days before the consultation.

Ms. Hunter's physician called the consultant and asked the consultant to speak with Ms. Hunter and her clinical psychologist friend, who had accompanied her to the hospital.

Process

The consultant received this urgent call from the surgical resident and went to the ICU, where medical students and house officers were gathered at the patient's side. After hearing the story from the chief surgical resident, the consultant went to speak directly with Ms. Hunter, as she was quite dyspneic and in impending respiratory failure. Her friend was available but chose to stay out of the room.

Physical exam showed a dyspneic woman breathing 30 times a minute on a rebreather mask in the ICU. With her mask off, Ms. Hunter spoke in clipped sentences. Her memory was excellent, and she said, "The most important thing . . . is to not . . . be . . . short of breath. I want . . . reasonable care . . . by reasonable doctors. I want to . . . make peace . . . with my family and friends." Ms. Hunter said that she didn't want to be kept on the ventilator if she became unconscious. The consultant did not discuss a living will with Ms. Hunter.

The consultant then spoke with Ms. Hunter's friend, who said that Ms. Hunter had not been in contact with her family for many years and had not wanted her family to be told about her admission. She was unmarried and not a religious person.

The consultant also spoke with the attending physician, who noted her recent change in heart from wanting to fight and recover to wanting to die. The attending also thought it was medically futile to prolong her life. The consultant provided a practical, peer-reviewed reference on relieving dyspnea in terminally ill patients.

Options

The consultant noted that when one can speak personally to a patient in Ms. Hunter's position, a living will is unnecessary. The consultant supported the attending's view that the prolongation of life was not a reasonable goal. However, the consultant pointed out that endotracheal intubation could be palliative and that its initiation "can be appropriate when the patient is uncomfortable, even in the dying process." The consultant endorsed the patient's request for reasonable care and suggested that such care might include intubating her for comfort to decrease her work of breathing and treating her with morphine, not to sedate her, but to decrease her dyspnea. The consultant also recommended contacting her family and friends and treating her aggressively while these contacts were being made.

Decision

After discussing the options with Ms. Hunter, her surgeons electively intubated her and began a morphine drip. Her surgeons agreed to changing the goals of treatment from attempted cure to short-term palliation. She was discharged from the intensive care unit.

Outcome

Ms. Hunter remained alert for days, and her friend called her family members, some of whom came to visit. On the fifth respirator day, Ms. Hunter died in a hospital room.

Summary

Again, the consultant acted in accordance with what the clinical circumstances asked: an urgent call from the surgical resident meant putting aside counseling a resident or writing a lecture and seeing the patient. The consultant attempted to be responsive, flexible, and patient-centered. Ms. Hunter's primary medical need for comfort made the ventilator a palliative tool in her case. The peer-reviewed reference given to house staff reflected the consultant's concern with the humanity of clinical practice. The consultant's assistance in judgment and in teaching was needed, as Ms. Hunter's illness was certainly terminal and there was little time to communicate. In terminal illness, the principles of hospice call for aggressive care and attention. Ms. Hunter's case was straightforward, in contrast to the case of Mrs. Bauer, whose illness was not certainly terminal, who had previously changed her mind about surgery, and whose family was present and opposed to her refusal.

Even without a reversible underlying disease process, the consultant's prompt attention to managing the case and teaching residents how to do so shows the value of respecting patient wishes and moving toward the goal of palliation.

JOE WANG

Question

"Are endoscopy and blood transfusion for this demented patient ethically proper when the patient's daughter, who is an attorney, objects?"

Case

Joe Wang is a 77-year-old man with endstage Alzheimer's and multi-infarct dementia who was admitted after physically threatening his wife. He was extremely agitated and was placed in a locked psychiatric ward. Twenty years before, he had had peptic ulcer disease and had undergone a gastric resection and jejunostomy. Two and a half years ago, he had had a large left-sided stroke but had recovered his speech and mobility. In the hospital, Mr. Wang's agitation diminished with neuroleptic treatment, but maroon-colored stools were noted on the ninth hospital day. A gastroenterologist could not determine whether the bleed was upper or lower and recommended upper endoscopy and blood transfusion. One of Mr. Wang's daughters objected, saying that her father was old and should be left alone.

On the day of consultation, Mr. Wang's hemoglobin was 8.9, down from 14.2 on the day of admission.

Process

The attending physician, a geriatrician, had arranged a family meeting on the day of consultation, so the consultant saw the patient with the attending, spoke with both briefly, and went directly into the family meeting.

On examination, Mr. Wang was alert, sitting in a chair being transfused; he had a 30-point orthostatic drop in his blood pressure. He refused a physical examination, and he denied being in pain, although his affect was worried and his mood was anxious. Present at the meeting were Mr. Wang's three daughters, his son, his wife, a geriatric fellow, and a nurse practitioner. It was noted that the patient had an arranged marriage of 40 years duration. No one remembered a specific conversation about advance directives for treatment, but the family members talked among themselves about whether they were doing the right thing in objecting to transfusion. They worried aloud that Mr. Wang was terminally ill, and that they were abandoning him. One of Mr. Wang's daughters, an attorney, produced a durable power of attorney for health care dated two months prior to admission. Mr. Wang had signed the form in three places. Mr. Wang's son asked, "When can we expect this to be over . . . for him and for us?"

The consultant expressed sympathy with the family's suffering. The consultant believed the durable power of attorney to be invalid, however, and pointed out that Mr. Wang could not have been competent to complete the form, given the advanced state of his chronic dementia. In light of this, the consultant suggested that Mr. Wang be transfused to an appropriate hemoglobin level and that endoscopy be performed as soon as possible. The meeting ended with the family promising to think over these suggestions.

Options

The consultant suggested transfusing the patient and performing a diagnostic endoscopy as soon as possible. Although diarrhea and transfusion reactions might result from the colon prep and blood products respectively, these should not be considered unreasonable harms, as the cause of bleeding might well be reversible. The consultant suggested not sedating Mr. Wang if he would cooperate with the preparation. The consultant also suggested continuing to discuss treatments with the family, with the goals of reasonableness and of not causing greater harms than benefits. The consultant wrote, "While the benefits/burdens calculus is not enough in many circumstances in the severely demented patient whose wishes are not convincingly known, it seems that a combination of this standard together with a reasonableness standard may well be valid."

Decision

Upper and lower endoscopies were performed, and the patient was transfused. The durable power of attorney was considered invalid but was not formally contested and was placed on the patient's chart.

Outcome

Both endoscopies were negative. The patient improved and was placed in a nursing home.

Summary

The consultant gathered data about orthostasis and the chronicity of the dementia and its effect on understanding and deliberation in signing legal documents. The consultant also questioned the use and manipulation of the patient by powerful, articulate family members. Mr. Wang's proxy was an attorney, who attempted to control the case; she was understood clearly from the start but was not confronted.

Confrontation may not always accomplish the patient's goals. When presented with an advance directive in circumstances of critical illness, clinicians have a moral responsibility to explore the directive.

Although deception by a family member is *a priori* wrong, it may be ethically justifiable to allow it to pass when personal care can still be delivered to the patient, the goals of treatment can still be achieved, and the patient does not suffer medical harm because of the deception.

In this case, the consultant judged these to be sufficient justifications to circumvent the question, What happens the next time Mr. Wang gets into medical trouble? A burdens/benefits calculus, clinical reasonableness, and negotiation techniques would again be useful. The document and the case were not subjected to outside legal scrutiny.

MICK FONTINO

Question

"Given this patient's family dispute and the girlfriend's apparent financial conflict, what is the proper course of action regarding dialysis and other life-sustaining treatment?"

Case

Mick Fontino is an 81-year-old man with a history of congestive cardiomyopathy, atrial fibrillation, and peripheral vascular disease. A femoral-popliteal bypass graft had been performed three weeks prior to admission, and Mr. Fontino had then signed out against medical advice because he "wanted to live on my own." He was readmitted with congestive heart failure and renal failure. On admission, he was confused and was unable to participate fully in decisions about his treatment. In the hospital, Mr. Fontino improved. The social worker, however, reported that his girlfriend complained that dialysis would "cost too much." The cardiologist asked the consultant to see the patient.

Process

Mr. Fontino had been a widower for 13 years. His girlfriend of 12 years lived in an apartment nearby, visited him nightly, and was prominently featured in his will. Mr. Fontino worked as a professional bookmaker and traveled annually to Las Vegas. He had two sisters whom he had not seen for eight years. Mr. Fontino's girlfriend insisted that he should not be dialyzed; his sisters, on the other hand, insisted that he should be dialyzed.

First, the consultant met with Mr. Fontino. On examination, Mr. Fontino was a supine elderly man who appeared chronically ill and was mildly confused. The exam was significant for a well-healed, left, above-the-knee amputation and bibasilar rales. Despite his bewilderment, Mr. Fontino's affect was appropriate as he said, "I'm not crazy—don't let them tell you that!" Mr. Fontino told the consultant, "I want to live as long as I can." He said that he was disturbed and frightened by the idea of dialysis and that it was difficult for him to make a decision. Mr. Fontino said that he was feeling better after initial hospital treatment and that he might not mind being dialyzed as long as he could still go to Vegas. He did not mention the existence of an advance directive.

The consultant then met with the family in a separate meeting, which was marked by acrimonious family fighting. Mr. Fontino's girlfriend complained that the sisters were uninvolved, uncaring, and opportunistic. The girlfriend called the sisters "vultures" and accused them of only being interested in the patient's estate. The sisters denied these accusations and said that the girlfriend was the "vulture." They said they were saddened by their brother's illness and wanted him to receive the treatment he wanted. The girlfriend insisted that Mr. Fontino would not want dialysis or any other life-sustaining treatment if he was "in his right mind," and she said that he was "out of his head." She said he was being intimidated by his physicians into accepting dialysis. Near the end of the meeting, the girlfriend pulled a legal document naming her as proxy from her purse and asked, "Can this help?"

The ethics consultant took the form to Mr. Fontino's bedside. The durable power of attorney had been signed by him during his hospitalization. His girlfriend was named as the agent. The most restrictive treatment plan (that is, a plan that rejects most medical treatments) had been checked by Mr. Fontino's girlfriend. When Mr. Fontino saw that his girlfriend had selected this treatment plan, he was surprised and said, "She did that. I signed it, but she did that. I want to talk about it with her. Why don't you come back later?" When the consultant asked Mr. Fontino why she might have selected this plan, he said that he had recently revised his will with her in mind, giving her a large portion of his $400,000 estate.

Options

The consultant recommended proceeding with Mr. Fontino's dialysis at his request, even though he possessed only partial decision-making capacity. The consultant also recommended rediscussing the advance directive carefully with Mr. Fontino when he regained full decision-making capacity, and finding a family counselor to address family conflicts.

Decision

The consultant's recommendations were taken, although Mr. Fontino's girlfriend complained to the attending physician and the consultant that they were violating his wishes and that Mr. Fontino was "out of his mind."

Outcome

Mr. Fontino improved after dialysis, and he returned home on dialysis ten days later. What happened to the durable power of attorney is unknown.

Summary

The consultant went back and forth between patient and family several times, and it was this action that helped to solve the case. This tenacity may be necessary when the medical details (dialysis and doubt about mental status) do not match the social and economic circumstances (a too eager proxy and uncertain motives). In a word, clinical judgment is central in attempting to understand why patients want what they do.

As in the case of Mr. Wang, a written advance directive was presented as a type of secret weapon by a significant other; unlike Mr. Wang, Mr. Fontino had decision-making capacity and, when given the opportunity, actively participated in his health care decisions.

Written advance directives can be ethically overridden when (a) there is evidence that the proxy is badly intentioned (rarely), (b) the patient's agent has considerable ambivalence about carrying out a patient's written wishes (occasionally), (c) the patient has a change of mind (sometimes), or (d) the patient has never discussed the clinical circumstance at hand with his or her proxy or doctor (unfortunately, often). Advance directives should be overridden when the situations in (a), (b), or (c) have occurred. For the most part, when the situation in (d) occurs, differences between patients, proxies, and physicians can be discussed, and agreement reached.

Proxies must make difficult medical decisions.

Uncertain Patient Proxies

WENDY SAWYER

Question

"Is it ethically obligatory for us to continue to care aggressively for an infant with short bowel syndrome whose parents are irresponsible and will not comply with provided therapy?"

Case

This is the twenty-eighth hospitalization for Wendy, a 25-month-old girl with gastroschisis and short bowel syndrome. Three months prior to admission, a laparotomy showed 30 cm of jejunum and transverse colon, without a ileocecal valve. Wendy was admitted for central line sepsis, had defervesced in the hospital, and had received parenteral nutrition but not gastrostomy feeding. Although she had a feeding gastrostomy tube, her parents had not been home to receive instructions for it. The consultant was asked to see Wendy regarding missed appointments, irresponsible parents, and questions of physician professionalism and responsibility. Blood cultures were positive for pseudomonas and strep.

Process

The consultant reviewed the outpatient records, examined Wendy, and spoke with her young mother. On examination, Wendy was a wan-appearing baby girl lying in a red play truck in her hospital room. Her temperature was 98.4°F, respirations were 32, and pulse was 128. Wendy's central line was intact, and a gastrostomy tube was in place. No abdominal tenderness was found.

Wendy's mother said, "I'm really concerned about Wendy not having a belly button." She described the home care personnel as "just upsetting Wendy" and cited numerous personal sacrifices she had made in caring for Wendy. She acknowledged that she had been investigated three times by the Department of Child and Family Services (DCFS), but she felt confident that she would always be able to care for her baby despite current financial and social difficulties. Mrs. Sawyer said that her husband, a security guard, worked long, late hours. She noted that it was difficult for them to meet the arranged home deliveries of total parenteral nutrition. She also acknowledged that her husband had threatened caregivers with a gun if they were to report them to the DCFS again, but she didn't think that her husband would actually become violent.

Options

Because of many documented instances of noncompliance with recommended treatment and because of Mr. Sawyer's threats of violence to caregivers, the consultant recommended involving the former DCFS caseworker in the discharge planning. Also, the consultant suggested that Wendy's physician write a one-page treatment plan/contract articulating appointments, visits, feedings, and expected progress toward nutritional goals. This plan would be shared with Wendy's parents, who had to agree to it for Wendy to receive continued care from the attending physician. The consultant also discussed the attending physician's own concerns about abandoning the child, as few doctors would understand the complexity of the case well enough to manage it.

Decision

The one-page plan was written by the physician, and the parents agreed to keep Wendy in the hospital for several weeks so enteral nutrition could be attempted. They agreed in principle to the plan. The attending discussed the case with house staff in a pediatric ethics conference, emphasizing the uncertainty of medical data, the limits of professional responsibility, and the importance of personal safety, especially when it was directly threatened. Resource allocation issues were not explicitly raised.

Outcome

Wendy returned home, but the parents missed numerous appointments. The hospital attorney recommended that Wendy's physician report the parents to the DCFS. Temporary custody was petitioned for by the hospital and obtained. A year later, custody was returned to the parents, but as another children's hospital had agreed to attempt to provide inpatient care, the hospital agreed to provide only emergency care.

Summary

The consultant played a less than central role in assembling the medical details in Wendy's case. As an internist, the consultant had to rely more on others' examinations and clinical work than in other cases. The consultant's primary role then became one of helping the physicians and nurses fulfill their responsibilities in caring for this very sick, helpless little girl and in educating her noncompliant parents.

Protecting vulnerable patients is a primary duty of the consultant, and this special charge is usually made easy by parents, who have the best interests of their baby at heart and in mind. In rare instances, parents can do no more, overcome by exhaustion, immaturity, poverty, or compulsion. In this case, the consultant acted as a counselor to the professionals more than as a counselor to the parents, as their problems were long-standing and probably could not be ameliorated by a short term visit, by codes, or even by the law.

Wendy's case was extraordinary, because her disease was complex, the hope for improvement was great, her vulnerability and dependence were considerable, and her parents were unable to cope with her illness or the medical system. Circumstances such as these must be balanced against not only the likelihood of harm to the patient, but also how much individual professionals and institutions can reasonably be expected to do—especially when what they know how to do is not enough.

GUADALUPE LOPEZ

Question

"Will you speak with this patient's husband, who is an attorney and wants to continue aggressive treatment of his wife?"

Case

Guadalupe Lopez is a 60-year-old woman with a 30-year history of a brain stem glioma. Fifteen months prior to admission, she had had a ventriculoperitoneal shunt placed after an intracerebral bleed. Having been discharged from the hospital just hours ago, she was readmitted from the nursing home with respiratory distress. She was returned to the emergency department, where her husband insisted on her reevaluation. An infectious disease consultant did not find evidence of pneumonia but, on the third hospital day, noted focal seizure activity, which did not abate for five days. During these seizures, she was intubated for airway protection. On the eleventh hospital day, the consultant was asked to speak with the patient's husband, an attorney.

Nafcillin-resistent staphylococci were growing in her blood cultures. A CT showed extensive tumor in the midbrain and brain stem.

Process

After being notified of the request for consultation by the attending physician's service, the consultant attempted to interview the attending, who only said that Mr. Lopez was a large and threatening man who was causing problems. The nurse complained that Mr. Lopez was belligerent and had made a co-worker cry.

The consultant asked Mr. Lopez to leave the room during Mrs. Lopez's examination. Mrs. Lopez appeared responsive to visual threat only and appeared to open her eyes when touched, but with the exception of the corneal and gag reflexes, her reflexes were absent. She had a gastrostomy tube, a foley catheter, an oxygen mask, and sheepskin booties.

Later, Mr. Lopez recalled discussing his wife's illness with her only once during its long history. She had said then, "I only want to do what everyone else can do." Mr. Lopez said, "My wife died on June 28, 1987. This woman is no longer my wife." He had requested that his wife be thoroughly evaluated because she appeared to be so uncomfortable. He agreed that the goals of care should be palliation and comfort, and he was disappointed by what he perceived as misunderstanding and insensitivity on the part of the medical staff. He noted that his wife was hospitalized for angina when she had her CNS bleed 15 months ago. The consultant spent several hours listening to Mr. Lopez's personal concerns and counseling him about his wife's care.

Apprehensions about dealing with Mr. Lopez, because of his large physical size and his potential ability to sue, were acknowledged by the consultant in discussions with the house staff. The consultant modeled good communication skills for the house staff, speaking directly and in a nonadversarial fashion with the husband.

Options

The consultant recommended a DNR order and the withdrawal and withholding of all treatments except for tube feeding, as Mr. Lopez had been apprehensive about this. The consultant suggested keeping Mr. Lopez informed, but counseled against turning decisions over to him. The consultant also noted that Mrs. Lopez should continue to receive comfort care and pain medications, if needed, so there would be no appearance of abandonment. The consultant wrote, "The fact that the patient's husband is an attorney should not change the treatment. The patient is dying and needs comfort care. We need to know the limits of medical care . . . "

Decision

The attending physicians stopped all diagnostic investigation and current treatment. No further laboratory studies were performed. The physicians considered adding treatments that might promote patient comfort but could think of none.

Outcome

After several days, Mrs. Lopez died in the hospital. In the interim, the doctors and nurses had spoken directly and without incident with Mr. Lopez. No suit was filed.

Summary

The consultant acted to integrate several elements of the case: the chronic, terminal nature of Mrs. Lopez's condition; the suffering of Mr. Lopez, husband and proxy; and the fear that the staff was forced to work under when Mr. Lopez was near. Encouraging and analyzing and being kind and gracious did more here than attempting to meet fire with fire and challenging the proxy to a legal duel. No principled, strident advocacy of Mrs. Lopez's rights would get her the care she clearly needed. In acting to help the patient, the consultant listened to both positions and acted as a liaison between them, discovering common interests.

Mrs. Lopez's case was very different from Mrs. Reichart's case. By using good communication skills and educating the husband about palliative treatment, the consultant helped Mrs. Lopez avoid over-aggressive end-of-life care. Differences in the personalities of family members and perceptions about family members' intent can affect the ethical outcome of a case. These were valid data to enter into the ethical analysis, but the snapshot quality of hospitalization (and often, of consultation) make these data highly subjective, something to recognize before making a judgment in a case such as Mrs. Lopez's.

PHILOMENA PERRINO

Question

"What is the best course of care for this woman who has had a severe cardiac arrest with brain damage, is in the ICU, and whose ex-son-in-law has physically tried to remove her from the ventilator?"

Case

Philomena Perrino is an 80-year-old woman from Italy who awoke with chest pain and left arm pain on the morning of admission. She was visiting her grandchildren and her American ex-son-in-law. In the emergency department, she was asystolic but was revived and transferred to the intensive care unit where a myocardial infarction and cerebral ischemia were diagnosed. While in the ICU, her ex-son-in-law physically tried to extubate her, saying, "I'm not going bankrupt for anyone! . . . All you're interested in is the money!" He demanded an EEG that afternoon, a Sunday, to prove that she was "brain dead." He had to be restrained by the hospital security personnel.

The next day, the risk management and legal departments were consulted. The hospital attorney suggested calling the ethics consultant, which the intensivist did that evening. Mrs. Perrino's daughter flew in from Genoa to meet with the consultant, her American ex-husband, and his attorney.

In the hospital, a large anterior myocardial infarction had been diagnosed on the day of admission. On the second hospital day, a neurologist found that Mrs. Perrino had an undefined left cerebral event and possible hemorrhage, with evidence of diffuse cortical and brain stem injury. A "Do Not Resuscitate" order had been written. The consultant was asked to see Mrs. Perrino on the fourth hospital day. No CT scan or other cerebral investigations had been ordered. Her medications included only ceftriaxone and vancomycin for septicemia and ranitidine for stress ulcer prevention; she had received no central nervous system depressants.

Process

The consultant spoke with the hospital attorney, who had received information from the risk manager, nursing supervisor, and a security guard about the ex-son-in-law's attempt to remove the ventilator. The consultant read their reports and then went to the ICU to see Mrs. Perrino while her daughter, ex-son-in-law, his attorney, and the hospital attorney waited.

On examination, the patient was comatose, on a ventilator, and normotensive. A neurologic exam showed an absent response to painful stimuli, fixed and dilated pupils, and absent doll's eyes, but it also showed spontaneous respirations and positive deep tendon reflexes.

The consultant then reviewed current literature on the survival of patients with anoxic encephalopathy and found that although Mrs. Perrino had a short clinical course, her prognostic category was already predictably poor.

In a long family meeting, the daughter said that Mrs. Perrino's sister had died barely three weeks earlier, after having been incapacitated by a stroke for many years. Mrs. Perrino had taken care of her sister, who was unable to speak, feed herself, walk, or dress herself. Mrs. Perrino had said many times that her sister would have been "better off dead . . . why didn't she die?" The daughter described her mother as a strong, independent woman who traveled freely throughout Italy. She wanted her mother to get better, even if the chances were ". . . one in a million." Mr. Perrino, hearing that Mrs. Perrino had become ill, had asked his daughter before she left Italy to find out how to make funeral arrangements while in America. The two attorneys, the nursing supervisor, and the ex-son-in-law did not participate in the conversation, although they were present during it. The daughter and her ex-husband did not speak to each other either. After the family meeting, at 1 A.M., the consultant and the hospital attorney telephoned the intensivist to report the results of the conversation.

Options

The consultant said that Mrs. Perrino was severely neurologically impaired, had a reliable, well-intentioned proxy decision maker (her daughter), and had expressed verbal directives regarding treatment for severe neurological disability that should be considered valid. The consultant did not discuss the ex-son-in-law's actions or motivations because those "initial concerns were, although unusual and dramatic, not of substance here and now." The consultant suggested that the intensivist discontinue life-sustaining treatment; the attorney spoke with the intensivist to support the legality of this action.

Decision

The next day, Mrs. Perrino was extubated by the intensivist. She breathed on her own and was transferred to a private room.

Outcome

The daughter maintained a vigil, and Mrs. Perrino died three days later. The hospital attorney counseled the attending physician. The patient's bill was paid by the ex-son-in-law.

Summary

The urgency of Mrs. Perrino's condition, the familial and cultural views that her daughter and ex-son-in-law brought to bear, and the referral of this case indirectly through the hospital's legal department combined to push the consultant to act quickly. Bringing current empiric data to the bedside, examining Mrs. Perrino carefully, and calling the attending physician to confer were key parts of the consultant's response to a critical, potentially inflammatory case. Levelheadedness, focus on the case at hand, and open-mindedness were valuable in helping all parties feel that they were treated fairly. Not addressing the financial and physical actions that actually brought the consultant to the patient was a strategy that attempted to focus on the real issues in the case: How sick was Mrs. Perrino? Might she get better? To what functional level over what period of time, and would she want to, given her values and motivations as understood by those who loved her?

This case illustrates the importance of emergent consultation when necessary, even at 1 A.M. It also illustrates that financial, social, and interpersonal motivations for decision making may not be readily apparent but may be clinically important to understand. The case turned on the personalness of Mrs. Perrino's past experience, the patience and steadfastness of her daughter, and the bedside participation of the hospital attorney, the risk manager, and a security guard.

ROD SINGER

Question

"Is it ethically and legally permissible to discontinue this patient's ventilator? If he dies, the other driver may be charged with manslaughter."

Case

Rod Singer is a 29-year-old man who had a severe intracranial and intraventricular hemorrhage in a motor vehicle accident. He was admitted with a Glasgow coma score of 3. The toxicology screen was positive for a cocaine metabolite, and his alcohol level was 0.285. In the hospital, the neurosurgeon found that Mr. Singer would not benefit from neurosurgery. Mr. Singer remains unresponsive on the ventilator. He has had high fevers and now has a left lower lobe infiltrate.

Mr. Singer was divorced two years prior to admission, and had a baby boy. His ex-wife remarried his best friend. Mr. Singer entered an alcohol treatment program. Sometime subsequently, he began drinking heavily again.

Mr. Singer had worked with his father in construction for 11 years. A few months before his injury, and in response to the severe neurologic injury suffered by two co-workers who had fallen through a broken scaffolding, Mr. Singer had said, "I would never want to be like that." The consultant was called about discontinuing of the ventilator.

Process

The consultant read the chart, examined Mr. Singer, spoke with the father separately, and then saw Mr. Singer again, together with all the family.

His medications included Librium, last given two days before the consultation. His last CT showed resorption of the hematoma in the right lateral ventricle. At the time of the consultation, an EEG was pending. A previous EEG showed encephalopathy.

On physical examination, Mr. Singer was comatose and on the ventilator. His temperature was 102°F, his pulse was 96, and his respiratory rate was up to 24 on an IMV setting of 10 breaths per minute. His pupils were slowly reactive, but he did not have corneal or gag reflexes. His extremities were flaccid and his Babinskis' positive.

The father told the consultant that he wanted his son "put out of his misery. . . . I wouldn't treat an animal like that . . . that's all he is now, an animal." He said that the patient's mother would "end up in a nut house" if Mr. Singer was maintained in this state, and that he would hold the doctors responsible for any psychological injury to his family that might result from a protracted course. Mr. Singer's father also said he was filing a suit against the driver of the other vehicle and that he wanted to set up a trust fund for his grandson with the monies obtained. The consultant spoke with the hospital attorney, who said that if Mr. Singer died, the other driver might be charged with manslaughter.

Options

The consultant advised a formal neurologic assessment by a neurologist to assess Mr. Singer's neurologic prognosis for recovery, a DNR order, and contacting the legal department of the hospital if the decision was made to forego life-sustaining treatment. The consultant also wrote, "There is danger of confusing the father's own distress and pain with that of the patient; the patient himself is not likely to feel pain and, in fact, as far as we know, does not."

Decision

These suggestions were taken. A neurologist found that Mr. Singer's repeat EEG was nearly normal and wrote in the chart that there was no reason for Mr. Singer's continued coma.

Outcome

A feeding tube was inserted, and Mr. Singer was treated despite his father's objections. Mr. Singer's neurologic status evolved to an awake, alert, locked-in state, and after three months and many more discussions with his father, Mr. Singer was discharged to a coma stimulation unit.

Summary

Even after the consultation was complete, many medical, personal, and social details were missing in this case: Mr. Singer's medical condition was uncertain; his father tried to displace his own anguish onto the clinicians; the clinicians doubted the father's competence, and worried about their potential liability for discontinuing life support. The consultant asked for a neurologist's expert assessment of Mr. Singer's neurologic prognosis for recovery. The consultant also knew that the clinicians' urge to help Mr. Singer was assisted by his young age but resisted by a grieving father, who felt that he had lost his son. The consultant wished to champion the patient's interest, but one statement made about someone else's accident seemed a shallow foundation for a life-and-death decision. Hoping that Mr. Singer could come back, and believing it too early to abandon hope, the consultant acted to help Mr. Singer survive, while sympathizing with his father.

Mr. Singer's case shows the necessity of following the patient and the role of professional colleague in the care of patients with complex clinical problems. The case also shows how the threat of legal action can be part of everyday decision-making and influence case management.

Students discuss a patient's choice.

I Decision-Making Capacity

MILDRED SLADKY

Question

"Can you persuade this debilitated but still spirited chronically ill woman to have a feeding tube placed?"

Case

Mrs. Mildred Sladky is an 81-year-old first-generation Polish immigrant with neurofibromatosis (Von Recklinghausen's disease) whose doctor has cared for her for ten years. She has been in a nursing home for three months. One year prior to admission, a cine-esophogram demonstrated chronic aspiration. Ten days before the consultant saw her, she was admitted with poor oral intake and persistent aspiration pneumonia. A pleural empyema was also found. Mrs. Sladky now refuses a jejunostomy tube. Because of the concerns of her daughter, who has also requested that Mrs. Sladky not be tube fed, the attending physician is asking whether tube feeding would be appropriate for this patient.

Process

The consultant reviewed the medical record, noting that a CT of the chest identified a probable lung tumor and that a speech pathologist had found moderate oropharyngeal dysphagia with all phases of swallowing. The consultant then spoke with Mrs. Sladky, who said that she no longer enjoyed the social aspects of eating. She disliked the idea of a feeding tube, and she knew no one in her nursing home who had a feeding tube. On physical exam, Mrs. Sladky was lying on her right side. She had a prominent left mandible and multiple neurofibromas. Her affect was sad. She appeared depressed, but her memory was excellent. She could only whisper answers to questions, but her answers were appropriate and clear. She refused a jejunostomy tube, but she did not refuse other treatments. She said that she was hungry.

Mrs. Sladky's daughter was interviewed. She said, "Food is very important to her . . . over the years, she saved scraps." She said that Mrs. Sladky is a first-generation Polish–American who immigrated with her sister more than sixty years ago. The daughter said that her mother had lost interest in many things over the last several years but still had maintained an interest in eating. She also noted that her mother had never previously refused any medical treatment.

The consultant returned several times to interview Mrs. Sladky, gathering more information each time and sitting close to her to understand her whispers.

Options

Despite Mrs. Sladky's depression, the consultant thought that she possessed decision-making capacity. The consultant suggested further treatment of her depression and a compromise: a jejunostomy and tube feeding for a limited period of time, and allowing her to sit up and eat even though she was aspirating. Otherwise, the consultant suggested that the staff respect her current wishes and provide hand feeding. In this case, the regular administration of small doses of narcotics was also recommended to decrease any potential discomfort.

Decision

The attending physician decided to offer Mrs. Sladky the compromise and accede to her wishes if she refused it.

Outcome

Mrs. Sladky accepted the compromise and took both J-tube and hand feedings. She returned to the nursing home after a thoracic surgeon performed a rib resection to allow the empyema to drain. Bronchial brushings of the apparent "tumor" were negative.

Summary

Good luck, persistence, and a willingness to research patient values combined to allow the consultant to synthesize patient interests (in eating and avoiding the debility that a feeding tube represents for many patients) and physician interests (in nutrition and avoiding patient debility too). Cultural and personal motivations for making decisions do not make a patient eccentric, and may make decision-making capacity easier to assess. In this case, the consultant took the time to understand Mrs. Sladky's motivations and acted to clarify common interests and work out a compromise. Agreeing on time-limited trials as a test of the solidity of a patient's otherwise shaky decision-making capacity gives credit to the patient and promotes goodwill.

The time spent communicating should enable consultants to be more persuasive rather than coercive. As in the case of Mrs. Bauer, Mrs. Sladky's case also demonstrates that many patients will accept therapy if they perceive it to be in their best interests and if it is offered on a time-limited basis. Like moral principles, decision-making capacity is not absolute: it should be assessed individually, for a particular task, and with wisdom. This case also shows that "probable" diagnoses of "cancer" are not certain diagnoses and that medical futility based on such a diagnosis may be flawed; unlike Mrs. Reichart, Mrs. Sladky did not have cancer.

WILMA SHELL

Question

"Can we transfuse this bleeding, critically ill, slightly confused Jehovah's Witness whose hemoglobin is 6 g/dl and who has been transfused before with her father's consent?"

Case

Wilma Shell is a 32-year-old Jehovah's Witness with acromegaly. She was admitted with upper GI bleeding and respiratory failure on the morning of consultation. A gastroenterologist was called, but Ms. Shell was too unstable to endoscope.

Process

It was Saturday and the consultant was at home when this consultation was received. First, the consultant spoke with the resident on call in the hospital, and then with the attending physician. The patient had had two craniotomies within the past 20 years for acromegaly, and her baseline mental status was intact but slightly confused. The consultant telephoned Ms. Shell's mother, who said that Ms. Shell had received a blood transfusion in 1979 with her father's consent. Ms. Shell's father is not a Witness, and her mother and father are separated. Ms. Shell's mother is a Witness, but Ms. Shell had never discussed the issue of blood transfusion with her mother. Ms. Shell's mother gave the consultant the telephone number of a church elder but would not reveal the number of her husband. She did not want her daughter to receive blood.

The consultant went to the hospital to see Ms. Shell; the resident was also present. According to the hospital fact sheet, Ms. Shell was a "Protestant." On examination, she was supine, on the ventilator, and receiving intravenous fluids. She had a blood pressure of 70/50, a pulse of 100, and a respiratory rate of 14. Her hemoglobin was 6 grams per dl. Ms. Shell appeared lethargic; she was able to squeeze the consultant's hand on command but was too ill to respond to questions about her religious convictions.

The consultant's telephone attempts to reach the church elder to inquire about Ms. Shell's beliefs concerning transfusion were unsuccessful. The consultant called a hospital attorney who had recently compiled for the medical staff a statewide case analysis of the treatment of Jehovah's Witnesses. Based on the admission data, the attorney questioned the validity of Ms. Shell's Witness status and advised that because of this uncertainty, administration of blood would be legally defensible.

Options

"If it can be verified that this patient is a Jehovah's Witness," the consultant wrote, "it would be ethically and legally appropriate to allow her to refuse blood." The consultant pointed out that if Ms. Shell's belief could not be authenticated, treatment should be provided. In the face of uncertainty about religious preferences, the medical indication for acute blood transfusion took ethical priority. References from a clinical ethics text were provided to the medical team, which supported the consultant's opinion that if "the patient's standing as a Jehovah's Witness [could not] be authenticated, treatment should be provided."

Decision

Ms. Shell became more hypotensive and was transfused with several units of blood that afternoon.

Outcome

Ms. Shell was endoscoped and had a large bleeding ulcer. She survived the bleed and was transferred to the floor. She was later told of the transfusion and was asked if her doctors had done the right thing. She replied, "I'm not sure." She did confirm that she was a Witness. She was discharged to a neurorehabilitation center.

Summary

The consultant was called for a clinical circumstance that could not wait. Given serious hemorrhage, suggested but uncertain religious beliefs, and permissive legal direction, the consultant advised transfusion, because further information gathering or negotiation would have been futile without the transfusion. Still, the consultant was wary of trampling on Ms. Shell's religious beliefs, which are often especially important in decisions near the end of life. Personal religious beliefs may be very different than doctrinal religious proscriptions. An effort to learn more about them (not the intention of promoting survival at all costs) grounded the beneficent action of transfusion in this case. The goal of restoring decision-making capacity also offered support for this action; while there was little doubt about Ms. Shell's inability to make decisions when hypotensive, it was still worth asking. Some consultants might have asked a court to review this case at the bedside, but the urgency of the patient's medical condition made this untenable.

FLORENCE VICK

Question

"Is it safe to let this patient return to her own home? The psychiatrist says she is incompetent."

Case

Florence Vick is a 69-year-old patient who lives alone and recently had an outpatient bronchoscopy for hemoptysis. Her internist related that she had adenocarcinoma of the lung, had undergone cranioradiotherapy, and was on high dose steroids. In the hospital, a psychiatric consultant said that Miss Vick had organic brain syndrome "probably secondary to metastases." Her hemoptysis had diminished considerably, and her appetite had started to improve. The oncologist was planning to send Miss Vick home until she said that she didn't allow anyone in, including a visiting nurse or Meals on Wheels messenger, and that she would do fine by herself. Her oncologist did not believe that she would do fine. Her medications included only iron tablets and prednisone. An MRI scan showed three enhancing nodules in the right cerebellar hemisphere.

Process

The consultant reviewed the chart and noted the MRI scan results. The consultant spoke to the nurse, who said that Miss Vick was doing better but that she seemed a little odd and had had no visitors. The consultant then spoke with Miss Vick.

She was unmarried, had no siblings, and said that she did not cook, but instead went to a restaurant every night. Miss Vick would not admit to having cancer. She said that she knew the topic of conversation and that it was uncomfortable for her to talk about. She noted that her appetite had improved since her 23-pound weight loss but said that she didn't want to think about either her illness or any further treatment she may need because "it may make me cry." When asked about other treatments, she said she would accept any except the feeding tube ("don't ask me why"). She saw no reason that she should not be allowed to return home. A man who worked for her had previously brought her restaurant meals, but now she did not even want him to visit.

On examination, Miss Vick appeared alert, pleasant, cooperative, and very thin. Her vital signs were normal. She had expiratory wheezes. No enlarged lymph nodes were palpable. Her remote memory, judgment, and insight were difficult to assess, but she was oriented, cooperative, and articulate.

The consultant spoke with the social worker, who said that Miss Vick's friend had reported that her house was a mess and that she could not possibly prepare meals. Miss Vick agreed, saying that she had never learned to cook and that there were too many hatboxes on the stove for her to get to it even if she wanted to.

Options

The consultant suggested discharging Miss Vick to her own home with supervision and recommended a trial of modified home care, giving her responsibility for fulfilling some duties. Suggested duties included taking medications, meeting nutritional goals, and keeping her appointments. Her physician's duties were to respect her wishes to live at home and to accept her refusal of tube feeding. Miss Vick did not have an obligation to accept home care, and while the physician's obligations did extend to providing care and assuring safety once she left the institution, Miss Vick herself would take responsibility for this. Finally, the consultant noted that while Miss Vick was eccentric and did not meet the didactic criteria for competency to refuse treatment (the ability to know and appreciate the disease, the treatment offered, the consequences of refusing treatment, and the alternatives to treatment, the ability to give a reason, and the ability to make a choice), she did have the capacity to make the specific decision — to return to her own home.

Decision

Miss Vick was discharged to her own home, without a feeding tube.

Outcome

Miss Vick went home but returned two days later throwing up blood; she died in the emergency room.

Summary

The consultant integrated a wide range of apparently conflicting data: Miss Vick had cancer but not cerebral metastases, as the psychiatrist had thought; Miss Vick had sought out medical care and accepted therapy for her disease, yet she would not call her disease by name; Miss Vick needed to gain strength by eating, but she appeared more concerned with privacy than with neatness or nutrition. The consultant's assessment of her decision-making capacity hinged on its particularity and on the pressures of her social circumstances and clinical condition.

Miss Vick's case illustrates the consultant's mandate to review carefully all available data in the medical record; for example, with her brain metastases being cerebellar, instead of cerebral, they were unlikely to alter her decision-making capacity, as was suggested by another consultant. Miss Vick's case also highlights the difficulty of balancing a patient's decision-making abilities against a particular principle, such as beneficence or autonomy.

VICTOR ADOMAVICH

Question

"Is it appropriate to allow this man to refuse blood transfusion?"

Case

Victor Adomavich is a 76- year-old previously healthy man who was admitted with a hemoglobin of 4.7 g/dl. This was his first hospitalization. Two days prior to admission, he had been seen in an urgent care center for a chronic cough; the laboratory had called him on the day of admission and told him to go to the hospital. He did not complain of fatigue, shortness of breath, melena, hematochezia, or weakness. In the hospital, Mr. Adomavich refused transfusion, complaining that "I might get AIDS or hepatitis." He was not transfused, and the attending physician called the ethics consultant. A cross-match of Mr. Adomavich's A+ blood type was compatible. The anemia was microcytic.

Process

The attending physician explained the case quickly to the consultant in the middle of morning rounds, and the consultant went directly to see Mr. Adomavich, without having a chance to review his chart.

On examination, Mr. Adomavich appeared pale and propped himself up on one elbow. His resting pulse was 110. His neurological exam was completely normal. Mr. Adomavich said, "I would rather have my own blood." He was surprised to learn that blood banks do not accept paid donations and that all blood is screened for antibodies to the HIV. He told the consultant that he is Czechoslovakian and had immigrated in 1948 under political duress. He is a published author and has been retired from the real estate business for six years. His wife died eight years ago of cirrhosis, and he believes that the physicians and nurses who cared for her were incompetent.

The consultant asked who Mr. Adomavich trusted, and he named his son, a professor of intellectual history in New York. While sitting next to the patient, the consultant called the son. Mr. Adomavich's son explained that hospitals in Czechoslovakia were places where patients went to die. He also described his father as having a "phobia" about people taking blood from him or giving blood to him. After the son hung up, the patient's phone rang again. When Mr. Adomavich stood up to answer it, he fainted, became diaphoretic, and was unable to speak for several seconds. The consultant helped him back to bed, and Mr. Adomavich said, "I have never fainted before . . . I am sure that not eating and the lack of sleep contributed."

Options

Despite possessing full decision-making capacity, Mr. Adomavich misunderstood the scientific risk–benefit ratio of a blood transfusion. Because Mr. Adomavich had no wish to die, the consultant did not believe Mr. Adomavich's fear to be a rational basis for refusal and suggested providing additional information about the goal of hospitalization and the intent of treatment. The consultant recommended that the attending physician enlist the help of Mr. Adomavich's son in changing Mr. Adomavich's mind. The consultant also suggested continuing to respect Mr. Adomavich's values and ideas and giving him time to talk about the transfusion.

Decision

Over the next 12 hours, the attending physician persuaded Mr. Adomavich to accept transfusion.

Outcome

Mr. Adomavich felt much stronger after transfusion, and a diagnostic workup was performed. A Duke's stage B colon carcinoma was found and resected successfully during the same hospitalization. Mr. Adomavich returned home to live independently.

Summary

Severe anemia is reversible, yet for a short time, it appeared that Mr. Adomavich's refusal of treatment would have untoward and unnecessary medical and personal consequences. Mr. Adomavich's decision-making capacity was never in question per se: he was always competent to make the decision at hand. Not until the consultant learned more of his personal, political, and medical fears, however, was Mr. Adomavich able to make an informed decision and the attending physician able to convince him that the risk of transfusion was small compared with the benefit (as of the late 1980s in the United States). Mr. Adomavich made the right decision; his decision-making capacity was not questioned, but supplemented.

While both Mr. Adomavich and Miss Vick apparently had decision-making capacity, Mr. Adomavich's disease etiology was unknown, therapy was undertaken easily, and risk was low. Miss Vick had a known terminal illness, for which effective treatment was not available. Drane has advocated a "sliding scale" for competency — demanding a high standard for refusals of life-sustaining treatment and a low standard for refusals of lesser treatments. Sliding scale efforts might also be considered when persuasion is needed. Persuasion and coercion, however, are on a spectrum, and the difference between them is sometimes impossible to discern.

JULIE CHANG

Question

"Please help us reason with this pregnant patient, who refuses a cesarean section, even if it is necessary to save the life of her baby."

Case

Julie Chang is a married 30-year-old G3 Ab0 P2 who is 40 weeks pregnant. She was admitted from the ultrasound department where her "bag of water" had broken that afternoon. The patient works at home and had wanted to deliver her baby at home, but her HMO did not allow it. She had only had one prenatal visit, at 26 weeks. Once in the hospital labor and delivery unit, her cervix was found to be 2 to 3 cm dilated, with contractions occurring every 2 to 3 minutes. She refused internal fetal monitoring and also refused to sign any of the consent forms for C-section or emergency procedures. She did accept external monitoring, which showed variable decelerations. She told the nurses that she felt the birthing process was more important than the health of the baby, and then she said, "I know I shouldn't feel like that." Laboratory examination results were pending.

Process

At 9 P.M., the hospital attorney, who had just referred the requesting obstetrician to the consultant, telephoned the consultant. The obstetrician wanted to go to court, but the attorney suggested that this was probably unnecessary. The consultant spoke with the obstetrician, who did not know the patient well and was grateful for any help. The consultant went to labor and delivery and spoke with the nurses caring for Mrs. Chang. The nurses described her as "bizarre" and were very concerned about the baby, especially if late decelerations should develop.

The consultant saw Mrs. Chang with her husband sitting in the room. On examination, Mrs. Chang was in labor, was using pursed lips breathing, and had an external fetal monitor in place. Fetal heart tones were between 150 and 170; the strip was flat, and contractions were regular.

Mrs. Chang said that she wished to have a natural childbirth. She said that if she had problems that threatened the baby's health, "I wouldn't have a choice, would I?" She said that she had worked as a volunteer in a pediatric emergency room during college, read Williams's *Obstetrics* during this pregnancy, and knew that internal monitoring was unnecessary. She also said that her first birth experience had been difficult: at 43 weeks, her labor had to be induced; she had wanted a girl, yet her first child was a boy. She felt like she did not participate in that delivery, and she said that she has not yet bonded with the child, now five years old. Two years ago, she delivered a girl at another hospital in a spontaneous vaginal delivery, without complications. She said, "If this baby is a boy, I'll give him up for adoption."

Options

The consultant pointed out that Mrs. Chang was fearful of invasive monitoring and medications like those administered during her first delivery. The consultant noted that her ambivalent and negative feelings about her delivery of that baby should be addressed later by a psychologist, as active labor was not the best clinical circumstance in which to address bonding issues. The consultant thought Mrs. Chang would consent to a C-section if it would save the life of the child. The consultant agreed with the attorney that legal intervention would probably not be required.

Decision

The obstetrician minimized further physical examinations and did not internally monitor the baby.

Outcome

Six hours later, Mrs. Chang spontaneously delivered a healthy baby girl; a day and a half later, Mrs. Chang went home with an appointment with a psychologist.

Summary

The consultant considered the immediacy of labor and delivery (late at night in the labor-and-delivery suite), the assessments of the experienced nurses, the constraints of Mrs. Chang's HMO (a red herring at the moment, but a factor to follow up on later), and Mrs. Chang's real psychological objection to the C-section. The consultant did not resort to legal threats or legal force, and again was engaged by the hospital attorney "to get the facts." The consultant worked in concert to facilitate what all hoped would be the outcome: the birth of a healthy baby.

As in the case of Mr. Adomavich, the use of persuasion was necessary to save a life. Also like Mr. Adomavich, Mrs. Chang appeared to have decision-making capacity in general, but the particular decision she made did not seem to fit the medical facts or even what was known of the social facts.

The consultant uses clinical judgment skills (not case management skills) to decide when and how to become involved in a case. This case illustrates a maternal/fetal conflict: a discussion of their respective rights is often polarizing and not the key issue. Mothers and babies are almost always on the same side, including Mrs. Chang and her baby.

MARYJO FOX

Question

"Is this patient competent to refuse dialysis, an operation, and other treatments? She says she wants to die."

Case

MaryJo Fox is a 66-year-old woman with avascular necrosis of the knee and chronic renal failure secondary to analgesic nephropathy. She has been dialyzed for five years. She was admitted with bright red blood per rectum. During a dialysis session two weeks prior to admission, Mrs. Fox had given her nephrologist a living will but had said that she still wanted CPR. In the hospital, she was found to have an ileal bleed, underwent subtotal colectomy, advanced to a full diet and began ambulating. She then complained of severe abdominal pain. A surgeon found a partial small bowel obstruction and recommended reoperation, but Mrs. Fox refused. She also refused further dialysis and said that she wished to die. Her medications included 4–6 mg of morphine subcutaneously every four hours as needed and 0.1 mg of Synthroid each morning. Her white count was 9,900, her BUN 85, and her creatinine 8.5. Her amylase and lipase were normal. Her family could not find her living will.

Process

The consultant spoke first with the floor nurses, who noted that Mrs. Fox's family was always present and that Mrs. Fox seemed very ill. The consultant read the chart: her ambulation several days before, her present refusal of dialysis, and her wish to die were all noted.

On examination, Mrs. Fox insisted that she was not depressed, that she had had enough surgeries and procedures, that she was prepared for an afterlife, and that her body was "worn out." Her clergyperson of many years confirmed that her statements were consistent with previous general statements about life-sustaining treatments and that she had a strong belief in an afterlife. Her husband of 48 years was supportive but tearful. No one could specifically recall her past wishes about treatment, although her pastor says that she had told him she would not wish to have any more operations, and that he is surprised she consented to surgery a week ago.

On examination, Mrs. Fox was alert and oriented. She was wearing mascara. Her memory was excellent, her cognition good, her mood reticent, and her affect frustrated. She did not appear sad, although she closed her eyes frequently during conversation. An abdominal exam showed positive bowel sounds, diffuse tenderness to light touch, a healing mid-abdominal scar, and right lower quadrant ileal conduit. Mrs. Fox's daughter insisted on staying with her mother throughout the interview and exam and asked the consultant to return the next day, when her mother might be feeling better. The daughter also insisted that the hospital respect her mother's wishes, as she had been "tortured long enough in life."

After speaking briefly with Mrs. Fox's husband, the consultant interviewed individually the rheumatologist, endocrinologist, general surgeon, dialysis clinical nurse specialist, and floor social worker. All agreed that Mrs. Fox seemed able to make decisions, and all knew that she suffered from endstage renal failure. The general surgeon was reluctant to accept Mrs. Fox's refusal of a reoperation, as it would take "30 minutes or less" to lyse the adhesions.

Options

The consultant found Mrs. Fox to be decisionally capable, depressed, and resolute about refusing a second surgery and continued hemodialysis. Recognizing that Mrs. Fox had a strong faith and a supportive family, the consultant suggested that the goals of care be turned toward comfort, including liberalization of family visits, patient-controlled analgesia, and an overall hospice approach. The consultant also suggested "keeping open the possibility of allowing Mrs. Fox to have an operation if she wishes to."

Decision

The medical team instituted a morphine drip and obtained a hospice consult.

Outcome

Mrs. Fox's bowel obstruction resolved. Five days later, on a Saturday morning, Mrs. Fox changed her mind and assented to dialysis as the attending physician said jokingly, "Ok, MaryJo, time for your dialysis." Mrs. Fox was dialyzed, went into disseminated intravascular coagulopathy, had a respiratory arrest, was intubated, and was placed in the intensive care unit. Mrs. Fox began to improve and then objected to some of the diagnostic and therapeutic procedures. The consultant suggested that despite her objections, aggressive medical care was indicated; the consultant also suggested a psychiatrist's consultation if she improved. Later, a psychiatrist found her to have a character disorder and prescribed psychiatric medication. Mrs. Fox went home two weeks later with nephrology follow-up and regular dialysis.

Summary

The consultant gathered information from key parties about Mrs. Fox's refusal of life support, and there was dissension from only her surgeon. Consensus was not enough here however, and the patient's expressed preference changed in critical illness, on the road to recovery. Hints at this sudden change included the contradictions uncovered vis-à-vis Mrs. Fox's living will; her ambulatory, never-miss-a-session dialysis visits; and her expected fatigue postoperatively. The consultant attempted to act to further Mrs. Fox's goals of avoiding more suffering, but she was still unsure of whether these were her most important goals.

The consultant erred in this case by recommending a hospice approach, but this error was not apparent until Mrs. Fox changed her mind. In assessing the decision-making capacity of such patients, the consultant should seek not only their ability to choose but also their reasons for choosing what they do. Patients may fluctuate in their decisions about life-sustaining treatment; certainty, however, is required when patients choose to discontinue life-sustaining treatment. Patients who change their mind often, or who make such decisions suddenly, may not be reliable decision-makers.

LOUELA STOKES

Question

"Do we have to get a second opinion for this schizophrenic patient whose daughter is requesting another opinion and a transfer to another facility?"

Case

Louela Stokes is a 74-year-old woman with a forty-year history of severe chronic schizoaffective disorder and a two-year history of gastritis and iron deficiency anemia. Two weeks ago, she was hospitalized in a locked psychiatric unit for self-destructive ideation and behavior, and she was treated with neuroleptics. Her condition improved. A social worker suggested placing her in a residential psychiatric treatment facility for continued treatment. Mrs. Stokes agreed, saying, "I need somewhere to live."

Mrs. Stokes's daughter, fearful that her recent erratic behavior would repeat itself, asked that Mrs. Stokes be transferred to another hospital for a second opinion about her mental illness. This daughter managed Mrs. Stokes's financial affairs; another daughter lived close by.

Process

The ethics consultant read Mrs. Stokes's medical record and interviewed the psychiatrist, the social worker, and Mrs. Stokes's nurse before speaking with Mrs. Stokes. The psychiatrist was fearful of a potential lawsuit brought by the daughter if the staff did not comply with her request; both the social worker and the nurse, however, believed that Mrs. Stokes was able to make her own decisions. Neither the social worker nor the nurse had met the daughter.

The consultant saw Mrs. Stokes. There was no history of weight loss or diminished appetite. Mrs. Stokes said that she did not need a second opinion and was satisfied with the care that she had received. When asked about her daughter's opinion, she said that her daughter had several serious psychological problems of her own, had ten children to feed, and "had her hands full all by herself." The patient's main concern was having a safe and quiet place to live. The consultant tried to call the daughter but could not reach her.

Physical examination showed a pleasant, slim woman sitting up in bed. Her temperature was 97.8°F, pulse 76, respirations 18, and blood pressure 120/80. Mrs. Stokes's weight was 104 pounds; her height was 61 inches. The examination was significant for a scaphoid abdomen that was mildly tender in the periumbilical area. Mild dystonic buccal movements were present. A mental status examination showed persecutory delusions. Speech was fluent and deliberate. There was no evidence of hallucinations, thought disorder, or impairment in cognition or recent or remote memory.

An admission hemoglobin of 11.2 grams had dropped to 9.4 grams the day before consultation. The mean corpuscular volume was 75 fls. An iron level was 23 mg, and a reticulocyte count was 0.9. One of two stool samples sent to the laboratory was positive for occult blood. An alkaline phosphatase level was 217 units/ml. Old charts did not show evidence of a sigmoidoscopy in the last several years, but not all of Mrs. Stokes's charts were available.

Options

The consultant's assessment was as follows: "This patient is able to make her own medical decisions regarding her placement and disposition when she leaves the hospital. Her ability to focus on the clinical issue at hand and exchange and understand information related to it is more important than neuropsychiatric testing or formal mental status examination."

The consultant suggested continuing to work up the anemia and look for records of a sigmoidoscopy within the last several years. If no evidence of a sigmoidoscopy was found, the consultant suggested performing it on this admission. The consultant also recommended that Mrs. Stokes be allowed to make her own decisions regarding health care interventions and, specifically, the location of discharge. To gain both daughters' support, the consultant encouraged their involvement in the formulated treatment plan.

Decision

Two days later, Mrs. Stokes's colonoscopy revealed a cecal lesion; the biopsy showed infiltrating adenocarcinoma. Through encouragement and reassurance, Mrs. Stokes consented to an operative procedure, a Duke's C2 lesion was removed, and adjuvant 5 fluorouracil and levamisole were administered.

Outcome

After several weeks of successful convalescence, Mrs. Stokes was discharged to a nursing home.

Summary

Patients with a psychiatric illness are often assumed to be incompetent to make health care decisions, but this assumption is not warranted. Like patients with dementia or a painful or critical illness, schizophrenic patients may be able to make some decisions. Mrs. Stokes's case illustrates the importance of assessing such a patient's decision-making capacity with care and in a nonthreatening, encouraging, and truthful way. The consultant tried to take in the whole case, not simply to answer affirmatively or negatively the question asked. The discovery of additional medical data in this case changed the ethical issues from place of disposition to whether to treat a malignancy and how to inform, support, and offer treatment for what could prove to be a fatal illness. This action was grounded in respect for Mrs. Stokes as a vulnerable, needy person. It was also made in the interests of all the clinicians in the case.

As in the case of Miss Vick, Mrs. Stokes's case shows that the consultant's curiosity about details can pay dividends; modeling this curiosity for others may teach them how to construct goals of treatment with a broad data base. Seeing the patient is ethically obligatory for the consultant: it is caring, expected, and potentially therapeutic. Otherwise, the consultant cannot effectively promote either patient autonomy or shared decision-making, both of which were critical for Mrs. Stokes.

Ethics consultation is knowing where to draw the line.

Should We Do More?

KRISTIE CONLEY

Question

"Is it appropriate to allow the discontinuation of peritoneal dialysis in this little girl who has a rare disease and whose parents are devoted but tired?"

Case

Twenty-one-month-old Kristie Conley has been hospitalized 18 times since birth. Developmentally, Kristie is at the one- to two-month level, although she has a social smile. She has non-vitamin B responsive methylmalonic acidemia, had a stroke three months prior to admission, and is dependent on peritoneal dialysis. Her current admission is for a temperature of 104.7°F and vomiting. Her blood cultures grew enterobacter cloacae, as did a sample of an intraabdominal fluid collection. In response to the parents' uncertainty that their child would survive much longer, the attending geneticist asked the consultant to review the case with them.

Process

After speaking at length with the geneticist, the consultant interviewed the night nurse about the parents' approach to their baby (attentive and loving). The consultant then spoke with Kristie's parents, while their healthy four-year-old ran around the room and Kristie lay in a crib. The parents were also caring for their two senile aunts in their home. Although they believed that dialysis and ventilators constituted extraordinary treatments, they had set up a mini-ICU at home; they mixed Kristie's formulas for her gastrostomy tube, supervised her hyperalimentation, and administered antibiotics.

On examination, Kristie was a chubby infant. She was awake, alert, and irritable. Her temperature was 99°F axillary; her abdomen was bandaged. The consultant reviewed the literature on her disease: only 100 patients with methylmalonic acidemia had been reported. Kristie's long-term prognosis was extremely poor and would likely include severe intellectual dysfunction. The consultant spoke with a pediatrician-ethicist about Baby Doe laws and reviewed the best interest standard for infants in the peer-reviewed pediatric ethics literature.

Options

Because the pediatrics team seemed to prefer a large, collaborative way of working through issues, the consultant suggested a staff meeting, including the parents, the attending physicians, the ethics consultant, a geneticist, and a social worker. The consultant also suggested that Kristie's parents and her physicians form an end-of-life plan seeking to limit treatment burden and that home health care be arranged. Trials of therapy, including mechanical ventilation and peritoneal dialysis, were suggested as options, but the consultant emphasized that "decisions to withhold certain life-sustaining treatments ought to be buttressed with decisions to provide comfort care."

Decision

After the meeting, a decision to write a DNR order and to continue peritoneal dialysis was made by the group. A home health care agency was contacted.

Outcome

Kristie was in the hospital for several weeks before she went home. She lived for eight more months, with many more hospitalizations. Her parents and physicians were reassured by the consultant's advice and support. Unfortunately, the parents divorced soon after Kristie died.

Summary

The consultant discovered Kristie's medical condition in a didactic way. The peer-reviewed literature and textbooks, however, could tell little about the good intentions of Kristie's parents or the nurses' feelings of care and love for someone so needy. The severe demands of chronic illness can literally divide families. Kristie's parents' divorce might have been predicted but was not (and could not have been) a key factor in deciding whether to limit treatment. Consideration of Kristie's best interests also included consideration of her parents' best interests, of Baby Doe laws, and of the cost of her care, which was picked up by two third-party payers. In this case, the consultant acted to consider Kristie and her parents as a unit.

This case demonstrates the importance of working within the values of the requesting specialty and team members and of considering the stress of a child's long-term illness on the family. Highly informed parents need help too — acknowledging and integrating the value of emotion in ethical decision-making is often part of this help. Consultants and families with highly analytical frameworks may benefit from such integration. Emotion may be generally understood as a missing link between rational, analytic systems and narrative, or story-telling, systems; but in each case, the role of emotion will be different and, in every case, can be thoughtfully undergirded by respectful listening.

OTTO KIEL

Question

"How can we provide for this patient's severe medical needs and get him home, where he wants to be?"

Case

Otto Kiel is a 71-year-old man with New York Heart Association Class IV congestive heart failure secondary to ischemic cardiomyopathy. He is bed bound and has been treated with intravenous dopamine and dobutamine for one week. Mr. Kiel has improved slightly in the hospital, but becomes hypotensive if the medication is stopped. He is presently being tube fed, is on nasal cannular oxygen, and wishes to return home. His medicines include furosemide (120 mg IV every eight hours), zaroxylyn (5 mg every morning), L-Dopa (250 mg every eight hours), captopril (12.5 mg every eight hours), and continuous intravenous infusion of dopamine and dobutamine.

Process

After reading Mr. Kiel's chart and speaking briefly with the attending cardiologist, the consultant interviewed and examined Mr. Kiel. On physical examination, Mr. Kiel was a dyspneic cachectic man sitting straight up in bed. He spoke slowly but had decision-making capacity. He wanted to continue to fight to live. Mr. Kiel's mother had died in her nineties on a respirator in the hospital. Mr. Kiel said that he did not want to be treated in the same way, which he termed "inhumane". He knew that he had only "a day or two, or perhaps a year or two." His fortieth wedding anniversary was one month away, and he mentioned living to this date as a short-term goal. He said that he had told several physicians that he understood his disease was terminal, and that he disliked the tubes necessary to keep him alive, but that he was going to continue fighting to live.

The consultant then telephoned Mr. Kiel's wife. She was concerned about the cost of home care. Mr. Kiel's intravenous cardiac medication would not be paid for by Medicare if he were to receive it at home. "It costs $300 a day — we can't afford that," she said. Mr. Kiel was prepared to sell his house to pay for this medication, but Mrs. Kiel didn't want to sell the house.

The consultant then spoke with the utilization review coordinator, who was on call that evening and knew of a hospital fund that might be available to pay for Mr. Kiel's medication at home. The coordinator agreed that, in the long run, home care was less expensive than hospital care.

Options

The consultant suggested seeking out this fund or, if it could not be found, finding another way to provide the medication. The consultant also suggested that the hospital might be able to waive its fee, if necessary, to provide resources for Mr. Kiel to live at home.

Decision

Mr. Kiel's physician made some initial arrangements to transfer Mr. Kiel home, and the utilization review coordinator began work on obtaining monies from the "innovative therapy" fund.

Outcome

Mr. Kiel died in the hospital the next day. He did not undergo CPR.

Summary

In this sad case, in which a terminally ill man would sell his house to live longer, the consultant actively sought out personal and familial information that might help him achieve his goals. Although unrealistic, Mr. Kiel's survival attitude seemed to give him energy far beyond what his barely moving heart could provide. While it may seem unfair to fight for some patients who are terminally ill, and not fight for others, it is the attending physician's and the consultant's specific charge to attempt to get the most appropriate treatment for each patient.

In this case, the consultant acted as a financial advocate and adviser to Mr. Kiel, empowering him to act as his own advocate and searching for resources to help him. In triage situations, principles of distributive justice dictate that resources be reserved for those who can return to the community to contribute, but Mr. Kiel was not being treated with direly scarce resources. Instead, as a patient searching for relatively scarce resources, he relied on his physicians' honesty and compassion.

HARRY O'DONNELL

Question

"How far must we go in treating and preventing a patient's advanced pressure sores? A plastic surgeon is advising amputation at the hip . . ."

Case

Harry O'Donnell is a 74-year-old nursing home resident who has been mentally retarded since the age of 10. He was admitted for sepsis secondary to an infected Stage IV pressure sore. He had flexion contractures of both hips and knees, chronic anemia, and a Stage IV decubitus on his left trochanter and a failed myocutaneous flap that had been attempted several months prior to admission. Then, the physician had attempted to secure a specialized bed to prevent pressure sore recurrence, but Medicaid would not provide the bed. The nursing home administrator, mindful of the home's recent citation by the state's Department of Public Health for the death of a Medicaid patient who had died of sepsis from an infected pressure sore, had demanded that the physician rehospitalize Mr. O'Donnell and provide more definitive therapy. The physician had complied.

In the hospital, Mr. O'Donnell's albumin was 2.6 and his hemoglobin was 10.1. Three organisms were growing from a culture obtained from one of the decubiti. A plastic surgeon recommended that Mr. O'Donnell undergo hip amputation or disarticulation.

Mr. O'Donnell has three sisters, one of whom is his legal guardian. He has lived in the nursing home for 14 years, feeds himself, recognizes his relatives, and watches television.

Process

The ethics consultant spoke with and examined Mr. O'Donnell and interviewed the attending physician, the surgeon, the primary nurse, and Mr. O'Donnell's three sisters, individually at first and then together in a large meeting. On physical examination, Mr. O'Donnell was an alert, pleasant-appearing man whose vital signs were normal. He was oriented x 1, smiled appropriately, and said "my hip" when asked if anything hurt. He had bilateral Stage IV decubiti and stiff, contracted legs and hips.

In speaking with the sisters, the consultant learned that Mr. O'Donnell had been independent in his activities of daily living and lived with his sisters in their home until he fractured his left leg 14 years ago and was placed in a nursing home. At that time, one of his sisters had become his legal guardian, but they had continued to make decisions for him as a group. Gradually, he had become nonambulatory, bedridden, incontinent of bowel and bladder, and increasingly confused. His retardation, they said, was the result of a car accident more than 60 years ago: "He just stopped like a clock; he has the mentality of a 10-year-old."

In a large family meeting, Mr. O'Donnell's sisters agreed that the overall goal of therapy should be to avoid burdensome treatments, a goal that the treating and consulting physicians believed to be attainable. The plastic surgeon proposed a hip disarticulation, and the sisters were sympathetic, wanting to give their brother "the best chance we can."

Options

The consultant highlighted Mr. O'Donnell's long survival, the wishes of reliable, well-intentioned proxies, and the uncertain achievement of the surgical goals of cure. The consultant recommended nutritional, hematologic, and rehabilitative evaluations, which focused on maximizing Mr. O'Donnell's intake of protein and calories. The consultant encouraged evaluation for the treatable cause of anemia and for any means of physically mobilizing Mr.

O'Donnell. To reduce the frequency of turns and of dressing changes, both of which appeared to make Mr. O'Donnell physically uncomfortable, an air fluidized mattress was suggested. The consultant also suggested that osteomyelitis, a contraindication to reoperation, might be present in Mr. O'Donnell's hip and should be ruled out.

Decision

These suggestions were taken. A hematologist found the anemia to be consistent with the anemia of chronic disease. Mr. O'Donnell's albumin did not improve with double portions, which he ate eagerly. A bone scan did not demonstrate osteomyelitis.

Outcome

Mr. O'Donnell returned to the nursing home without an operation. Poorly responsive and septic, he returned to the hospital almost a year later. Another surgeon operated and debrided the ulcers emergently, and Mr. O'Donnell eventually returned to the nursing home.

Summary

The starkness of severe pressure sores is upsetting to clinicians and families alike when the pressure sores are actually seen (which isn't often, as they are usually posterior, and covered by bandages, bed covers, or clothes). Health care professionals and their institutions are often stigmatized by the occurrence of pressure sores even though they can occur in the natural history of some diseases. In this case, the consultant researched the pressure sore literature for data on the prognosis for healing and recurrence, learned about Mr. O'Donnell's caring sisters, and attempted to temper an automatic, technical response to cover up sores that almost certainly would not heal. Little meaningful personal data could be gathered, and it was primarily a sense of realism that permitted the consultant to advise against aggressive surgical care. Such treatment is often inconsistent with the overall goals of therapy in immobile patients.

As in the case of Mr. Kiel, Mr. O'Donnell's case showed how doctors could appeal economic constraints in a patient's care and how the consultant could facilitate these appeals. Private and public funding for effective prevention and early treatment were restricted and constrained. Unlike Mr. Kiel's case, however, Mr. O'Donnell's doctors did not all agree on the proposed treatment, Mr. O'Donnell's disease was not classically terminal, and treatment was not classically life sustaining.

VITO CONSOLI

Question

"Can this patient refuse to eat but still accept a gastrostomy tube? Can we simply allow him to refuse?"

Case

Vito Consoli is an 81-year-old man who had had a pacemaker implantation two years ago. Two weeks before his current admission, he had suffered a left parietal stroke. He had been transferred from an outside hospital for further rehabilitation. He had been in the hospital for nearly two weeks and was found to have a nonfluent expressive aphasia, a swallowing dyspraxia, and mild clinical depression. He refused a percutaneous gastrostomy tube. A gastroenterologist noted that Mr. Consoli found his present condition unacceptable, and suggested an ethics consultation. For the past week, Mr. Consoli has received Tofranil, as suggested by a psychiatrist.

Process

The consultant reviewed the chart and spoke first with the rehabilitation physician, who thought that Mr. Consoli's stroke was so massive that it might be terminal. The consultant then saw Mr. Consoli. On examination, Mr. Consoli was an alert, sad-appearing man sitting in the wheelchair. His vital signs were normal. He refused further exams, nodded and shook his head appropriately, and attempted to write with his left hand.

The consultant then met with Mr. Consoli's son and daughter-in-law, who said that Mr. Consoli's wife did not know how ill he was; they did not plan to tell her, because it would frighten her. His wife has a newly diagnosed neoplasm and was receiving radiation therapy.

Mr. Consoli was described as a kind, accepting man, who retired as a mold maker more than 20 years ago. He spoke Italian and French, but little English. His son and daughter-in-law lived downstairs. When confronted with the need for a pacemaker two years before, Mr. Consoli had asked, "Will I be able to work in the garden?" His daughter-in-law had assured him that he would, and the pacemaker had been implanted and had functioned without complication. To encourage him to eat, his daughter-in-law had brought his favorite minestrone and cut up pasta from home, but Mr. Consoli did not eat. The son said that he had asked Mr. Consoli in Italian, "Why won't you eat, Pop?" Mr. Consoli had replied in Italian, "It doesn't taste good." Mr. Consoli had said many times, "When my time is up, it's up. That's it."

The consultant then observed the daughter-in-law with Mr. Consoli. She said, "Dad, don't you want to eat? Eat, eat, eat, eat." She was insistent, hounding him, and he ate a french fry as the ethics consultant watched.

Options

The ethics consultant wrote, "This patient does not offer a reason for refusing treatment, in part because of his expressive aphasia and perhaps in part because his health care givers are not asking the question in Italian. When food doesn't taste good, it may be due to organic illness, depression, or food quality or methods of preparation. No evidence exists that Mr. Consoli refuses to eat because of prior conviction, advance directive, or quality of life considerations. He apparently refuses to eat because the food doesn't taste good and because depression may be affecting his decision making. How do we know this? We may not, until three weeks of antidepressants are given." The consultant suggested communicating through the son in Italian when possible, and beginning gastrostomy feedings until Mr. Consoli improved.

Decision

The decision was made not to insert a gastrostomy tube, and Mr. Consoli was continually encouraged to eat, especially by his daughter-in-law.

Outcome

Mr. Consoli was treated for clinical depression, given food from home made by his daughter-in-law, and spoken to in Italian. He returned home after several days to the care of his family.

Summary

The consultant learned and acted by observing. The rehabilitation physician's assessment of Mr. Consoli's poor ability to recover an appetite took into account only his disease process and not the cultural and familial ties that were so dear or the language barrier that actually prevented clear communication. The consultant asked the question "Why?" when faced with an apparent refusal of treatment and "Why not?" when a colleague wished not to give more treatment. Again, drive and determination pushed the clinical circumstances along, and the consultant only had to watch and not be too eager to discontinue treatment or to take up (at the moment) peripheral issues, such as whether, when, and how to tell Mr. Consoli's wife his prognosis.

This case demonstrates the importance of a family member who is very interested (even pushy) in a patient's care; the daughter-in-law made this convalescing patient eat. Contrast Mr. Consoli's case to that of the critically ill Mrs. Bauer, whose family did not want her to give up but did not feel able to intercede — there, the doctors made the difference. When is it ethically justified to push a patient? When a patient can get better, when a patient is not acting like himself or herself, and when a patient has something for which to live. How people will act when they are patients is hard to predict and, in each case, is best ascertained at the bedside. Here, the daughter-in-law just knew how to treat her father-in-law.

YOLANDA CISTERNA

Question

"Did I do the right thing in threatening to tell this manic patient's parents that she wants to have an abortion?"

Case

Yolanda Cisterna is a 22-year-old woman with a diagnosis of bipolar affective disorder. She was admitted to a locked psychiatric ward after she had attempted to hot-wire cars and overtly proposition strangers. Over her five-week hospital stay, she has been treated with tegretol and haldol, instead of lithium, because she wished to avoid weight gain. She became calmer and more compliant after treatment, but one month after admission, it was discovered that she was pregnant. A pregnancy test on admission had been negative. The patient said that she had been raped several days prior to admission and told her psychiatrist that she wished to have an abortion. She asked her psychiatrist not to tell her parents and to help her get an abortion. The psychiatrist said, "You may not be able to make your own decision on this . . . I can't keep this information confidential. I think keeping it secret from your parents would be unwise." On the following day, Ms. Cisterna changed her mind and decided to keep the baby.

Process

The consultant reviewed the chart. An HIV test was negative. An ultrasound showed a five-week pregnancy with no fetal pole visualized. The consultant then spoke with an obstetrician colleague, who advised that about one-quarter of viable pregnancies do not have a visualized fetal pole at five weeks and that serial HCGs would show whether the fetus was growing. The consultant asked the drug information division for a review of the teratogenicity of Ms. Cisterna's medications, which showed adverse first-trimester effects of lithium and unknown effects of tegretol and haldol.

The consultant interviewed Ms. Cisterna alone, her parents alone, and then all of them together with the psychiatrist, the psychiatric resident, and the clinical ethics nurse. Ms. Cisterna had never before been pregnant. She was not married and lived at home with five brothers and sisters. She did not work and had attended beauty college for two years. Ms. Cisterna said that her sister had told her it would be a crime to have an abortion. In the large meeting, her parents said that they would care for the baby. "What's one more?" they asked. When the psychiatrist suggested that her parents would love her even if she decided to have an abortion, Ms. Cisterna said that she needed a couple of days to think about it.

Options

The consultant discussed the case at length with the attending physician. The consultant understood the attending's reason for threatening to breach confidentiality but did not think trust could be improved by doing so. The consultant outlined a number of choices, such as performing a quantitative HCG measurement to verify fetal viability and contacting Ms. Cisterna's Spanish-speaking outpatient therapist to counsel her about her pregnancy options. The consultant acknowledged the family's religious opposition to abortion and also recommended regular appointments to assess Ms. Cisterna's decision-making capacity and to determine tegretol levels. Even though Ms. Cisterna might make better progress on lithium, the consultant suggested that because of its teratogenicity, it should not be used in the first trimester. A second-trimester trial of lithium was recommended if Ms. Cisterna's decision-making capacity had not improved. The consultant also suggested that the parents become her legal guardians for her safety if she was unable to regain decision-making capacity.

Decision

Ms. Cisterna was treated as an inpatient for another week. Two HCGs three days apart were obtained; the titer was rising, indicating a viable fetus. Ms. Cisterna's parents did not become her legal guardians but promised to care for the baby when he or she was born. Yolanda returned home and had regularly scheduled office visits with her psychiatrist.

Outcome

Two weeks after discharge, Ms. Cisterna changed her mind again, after having seen the psychiatrist in the office once. The psychiatrist referred her to an obstetrician, and she underwent an abortion.

Summary

This dramatic case came after the fact: the psychiatrist had said something and, being unsure whether it was right, wanted a second opinion. The consultant could still help the psychiatrist appreciate the dimensions of the problem and, to do that, gathered data about

Ms. Cisterna's pregnancy, psychosis, fears, and maturity. Guiding the consultant's action was concern for Ms. Cisterna: what would help her most, as she understood it, about this pregnancy?

Language and cultural barriers made communication more difficult but, in the end, still possible; and the question of doing more arose not only for the patient but for a significant (soon-to-be) other. The consultant acted to counsel the psychiatrist in private about the breach of confidentiality (perhaps permissible, as Ms. Cisterna clearly wanted and needed the support of her parents in either keeping or giving up the pregnancy) and to counsel Ms. Cisterna in a group with her family.

This case also revealed the difficulty a patient could have with fluctuating decisional capacity. The consultant urged Ms. Cisterna's parents to become her guardians, but they were unwilling to assume this responsibility. Ms. Cisterna changed her mind several times about whether to have the abortion. Even while the consultant did not agree with the psychiatrist's actions, the consultant worked as a professional colleague with the psychiatrist. In the end, Ms. Cisterna made her own decision to have an abortion.

ARTURO DINERRO

Question

"What are our responsibilities in caring for this neurologically injured patient who tries to bite us, is HIV positive, and is an illegal alien?"

Case

Arturo Dinerro is a 26-year-old Guatemalan who entered the hospital two months ago after he had suffered a closed head injury in a motor vehicle accident. He had subdural and subarachnoid hemorrhages and required mechanical ventilation. He tested positive on admission for alcohol, opiates, and the HIV antibody, and he was given AZT in the hospital. His HIV risk factors were unknown. Since his injury, he has been confused, and the nurses have reported that he frequently spits and occasionally tries to bite. He is married, has worked at a gas station for ten years, and has a 4-year-old daughter.

He also has a 9-year-old son from a previous relationship. His family members know that he is HIV positive; his wife and daughter have been tested and are negative.

The laboratory exam showed HIV positivity, a WBC of 3,400, a hemoglobin 9, and adequate platelets. Mr. Dinerro is on AZT, mellaril, haldol, and tegretol.

Process

The consultant spoke with the floor nurse who complained about Mr. Dinerro's abusive verbal and physical behavior. Then the consultant reviewed the chart and saw Mr. Dinerro. He was oriented x 2, was agitated, and writhed in bed in four-point restraints. Vital signs were normal, but he could not be examined because he would not cooperate. He spoke primarily in English and seemed to understand what the consultant said, but he also spoke gibberish and spit into the air. Mr. Dinerro asked if the consultant would like to have a beer, but the consultant declined, saying that it was early in the morning. Mr. Dinerro encouraged the consultant to have one anyway. Mr. Dinerro asked the consultant not to ask about being HIV positive or his drug use and to release him from his restraints.

The consultant then interviewed Mr. Dinerro's wife, who expected her husband to return home after rehabilitation.

Options

The consultant suggested that the goals of care should be to restore physical function, if possible, while adequately protecting the staff from injury. The consultant suggested using medical data as a guideline for therapy and consulting with Mr. Dinerro's wife as his proxy since Mr. Dinerro was incapacitated. The consultant also suggested retesting the daughter and wife for HIV and pursuing Medicaid and social security disability. The consultant discussed the concept of professional responsibility with the nurses, empathizing with them but stressing that Mr. Dinerro was not in control of his actions, probably as a result of his injury. The issues of financial cost to the institution and foreign citizenship were raised, and although important, they were considered to be less important than the mission of addressing present patient needs.

Decision

The doctors and nurses continued treating Mr. Dinerro. They were disappointed that the consultant seemed to take the patient's side but accepted the consultant's suggestions.

Outcome

Mr. Dinerro eventually went to the rehabilitation unit, where he lived for four months before being discharged home; he was able to ambulate. All of the family members were HIV negative.

Summary

Ethical issues in the HIV disease continue to evolve, and the dilemmas of privacy, truth-telling, professionalism, and uncertainty in medicine were all evidenced in this case. The consultant's actions were grounded in sympathy for the caregivers, who had other patients to care for and who wanted to avoid injury themselves. The consultant also attempted to protect an indigent Hispanic man with a critical illness. The attending physician disagreed with the consultant's advice to continue treatment, but did so anyway. The consultant encouraged this action and attempted to limit abuse of the patient, who, after all, could do little to help himself.

As in the case of Wendy Sawyer, the case of Mr. Dinerro showed that the health care team could encounter the threat of physical harm at work. Unlike Wendy Sawyer's case, however, the case of Mr. Dinerro showed that hazard to be an occupational risk, instead of an avoidable injury. Being in a profession that serves a public good and favors altruism over self-interest, carries responsibilities for competency and compassion; these responsibilities, in turn, create a high standard for behavior.

Annotated Bibliography

CASE CONSULTATION

Anzia, D. and J. La Puma. "Right Action: Practical Reasoning in Medicine." *J Clin Eth* 1, no. 3 (1990):193–94.

The authors use a case to show how and why the consultant is obligated to make a competent assessment of the goals of care, as well as to suggest a means of achieving these goals.

Caplan, A. "Can Applied Ethics Be Effective in Health Care and Should It Strive to Be?" *Ethics* 93 (1983):311–19.

The author is critical of the "engineering model of applied ethics," warning that "moral efficacy is desirable only when the right questions are being addressed."

Doukas, D. "The Design and Use of the Bioethics Consultation Form." *Theor Med* 13 (1992):5–14.

A family physician gives a theoretical framework for outlining salient principles in ethics consultation. Testing of the framework is advocated.

Edinger, W. "Which Opinion Should a Clinical Ethicist Give: Personal Viewpoint or Professional Consensus?" *Theor Med* 13 (1992):23–29.

Consultants may occasionally be called upon to give a consensus view that differs from their own personal analysis of the clinical circumstance at hand. The consultant should outline the arguments supporting each position and allow the requesting physician to choose.

Edwards, M., and S. Tolle. "Disconnecting a Ventilator at the Request of a Patient Who Knows He Will Then Die: The Doctor's Anguish." *Ann Intern Med* 117 (1992):254–56.

Two ethics consultants describe their direct involvement in a terminally ill patient's case, and their clinical, personal, and emotional reactions to insuring that ventilator withdrawal was right for the patient.

Fletcher, J. "The Goals of Ethics Consultation." *Biolaw* 2, no. 2 (1986): 36–47.

An important, early paper in which Fletcher suggests five models of consultation and a list of criteria for what may constitute an ethics consultation process.

Kass, L. "Practicing Ethics: Where's the Action?" *Hast Cent Rept* 20, no. 1 (1990):5–12.

Scholar and statesman Kass concludes that if ethics is to be meaningful in health care, it must return to the bedside of individual patients.

La Puma, J. and D. Schiedermayer. "Must the Ethics Consultant See the Patient?" *J Clin Eth* 1, no. 1 (1990):56–59.

The case of an elderly woman with chronic schizophrenia and colon cancer is presented to show that the consultant must go to the bedside and see the patient to discover necessary information. The discussion includes ten reasons for seeing the patient.

La Puma, J., C. Stocking, C. Darling, and M. Siegler. "Community Hospital Ethics Consultation: Evaluation and Comparison With a University Hospital Service." *Amer J Med* 92 (1992):346–51.

The authors compare 104 community hospital consultations performed by a single consultant over two years with 51 consultations performed by an ethics consultations service in a teaching hospital over one year. Requesting physicians found the consultations helpful in ethics education and in case management.

La Puma, J., C. Stocking, M. Silverstein, A. DiMartini, and M. Siegler. "An Ethics Consultation Service in a Teaching Hospital: Utilization and Evaluation." *JAMA* 260 (1988):808–11.

A prospective evaluation of an ethics consultation service at a large academic institution that had documented the nature of 51 requests received. The majority (96 percent) of the requesting physicians were satisfied with the consultation process and indicated that they would request another consultation.

Miles, S. "Informed Demand for 'Nonbeneficial' Medical Treatment." N Engl J Med 325 (1991):512–15.

An experienced internist/consultant attempts to balance the attorney/husband's demand for all medical care for his ventilator dependent, PVS-burdened wife with the county institution's commitment to the medically indigent. The husband asks the consultant to manage the case, even though the consultant objects to the husband's petition for guardianship.

Orr, R., and C. Moon. "Effectiveness of an Ethics Consultation Service." J Fam Pract 36, no. 1 (1993):49–53.

Sixty-one patients, most of whom were children in critical care in a university hospital, were seen over a year's time, and retrospectively reviewed; satisfaction of requesting physicians was very high.

Perkins, H. "Another Ethics Consultant Looks at Mr. B's Case: An Ethical Dilemma." J Clin Eth 1, no. 2 (1990):126–32.

In a thorough and detailed analysis, Perkins dissects the ethical issues in Mr. B's case and models clear, critical analysis for consultants and committees.

———, and B. Saathoff. "Impact of Medical Ethics Consultations on Physicians: An Exploratory Study." Amer J Med 85 (1988): 761–65.

Most of these 44 ethics consultations involve patients' decisional capacity regarding the right to refuse treatment or the right of proxies to refuse treatment.

Perl, M. and E. Shelp. "Psychiatric Consultation Masking Moral Dilemmas in Medicine." N Engl J Med 307 (1982):618–21.

Because requests for moral advice were often referred to psychiatrists, psychiatrists were the earliest ethics consultants. The authors

describe their recognition of this dilemma and suggest the development of a new expertise in medicine to resolve it.

Pruzinsky, T. "Definition and Evaluation of Biomedical Ethics
Consultation: An Annotated Bibliography." *Society for Bioethics
Consultation Newsletter* 1, no. 2 (1989):3–7.
    Three-paragraph summaries of published and unpublished arti-
cles known to the editor, who is a clinical psychologist in a university
department of plastic surgery and a consultation service member.

Purtilo, R. "Ethics Consultations in the Hospital." *N Engl J Med*
311 (1984):983–86.
    One of the first reports, this analysis uses the author's reflections
on a case she saw that morning to reflect on the proper role for
consultants and whether consultants ought to be paid.

Rodeheffer, J. "Practical Reasoning in Medicine and the Rise of
Clinical Ethics." *J Clin Eth* 1, no. 3 (1990):187–92.
    A sophisticated, philosophical analysis of the nature of practical
reasoning and clinical judgment. The author suggests that consultants can develop a specialized practical reasoning through training
and experience; as a necessary conclusion, action follows directly.

Self, D., and J. Skeel. "A Study of the Foundations of Ethical
Decisionmaking of Clinical Medical Ethicists." *Theor Med* 12
(1991):117–27.
    Philosophers and theologians who perform ethics consultations
may apply principle and theory to cases, but often they are drawn to
the details of cases to illustrate principle and theory.

Siegler, M. "Clinical Ethics and Clinical Medicine." *Arch Intern
Med* 139 (1979):914–15.
    The author, director of the largest training program in clinical
ethics, notes that clinical ethics is focused on the practical everyday
concerns of patient and doctor. He cautions against armchair ethics.

——. "A Legacy of Osler: Teaching Clinical Ethics at the Bedside." *JAMA* 239 (1978):951–56, and E. Pellegrino. "Ethics and
the Moment of Clinical Truth." *JAMA* 239 (1978):960–61.

Both Siegler and Pellegrino advocate the bedside teaching of clinical ethics. Siegler advocates teaching ethics like Osler taught medicine, and Pellegrino argues that ethicists and clinicians must find a common language.

Siegler, M., and P. Singer. "Clinical Ethics Consultation: Godsend or 'God Squad'?" Amer J Med 85 (1988):759–60.
Cautionary advice to clinicians who undertake consultation, reasoning that the legal, medical, and moral authority for a patient's management remains with the attending physician and urging the prospective evaluation of ethics consultation.

Simpson, K. "The Development of a Clinical Ethics Consultation Service in a Community Hospital." J Clin Eth 3, no. 2 (1992): 124–30.
The author analyzes 59 requests for consultations received over two years in a university affiliated, urban community teaching hospital. Simpson also tells of his struggles with acceptance in this environment, and helpfully reviews his methods for data gathering, and for training as a clinical ethicist.

Smith, D. "Telling Stories as a Way of Doing Ethics." Connecticut Med 51, no. 11 (1987):725–31.
Patient stories can be understood as parables or fables, if those involved play important, evolving parts within these stories. Patients' stories speak of their humanity and enrich clinicians' framework for understanding ethics beyond the bounds of principle, rule, or virtue.

Tulsky, J., and B. Lo. "Ethics Consultation: Time to Focus on Patients." Amer J Med 92 (1992):343–45.
Ethics consultation services are "promising experiments." Research in clinical ethics consultation should take advantage of the methodologies of clinical epidemiology and decision analysis, as well as assess patient satisfaction.

Wear, S., P. Katz, B. Adrzejewski, and T. Haryadi. "The Development of an Ethics Consultation Service." HEC Forum 2, no. 2 (1990):75–87.

Ethics consultation services can find accountability and legitimacy within the structure of an institutional ethics committee.

Webb, W. "The Ethics of the Consultation Process." *Psychosomatics* 28 (1987):278–79.
The consultant has an ethical obligation to follow up.

TRAINING, SKILLS, AND CERTIFICATION

Barnard, D. "Reflections of a Reluctant Clinical Ethicist: Ethics Consultation and the Collapse of Critical Distance." *Theor Med* 13 (1992):15–22.
Ethics consultants who are not clinicians by training can use this distance to maintain perspective and their own identity when viewing the clinical setting.

Beeson, P. "The Natural History of Medical Subspecialties." *Ann Intern Med* 93 (1980):624–26.
A short authoritative review of the evolution of fields of expertise in internal medicine.

Benson, J. "Certification and Recertification: One Approach to Professional Accountability." *Ann Intern Med* 114 (1991):238–42.
Assessment and accountability are acceptable as modern watchwords in medicine; in internal medicine, certification serves as a mark of academic distinction and clinical qualification. Voluntary recertification is highly desirable as a measure of professional and public credibility.

Cassel, C. "Certification: Another Step for Geriatric Medicine." *JAMA* 258 (1987):1518–19.
Specialization is a mixed blessing, but on balance, it can lead to improved patient care. Collaboration between family medicine and internal medicine have resulted in a mutually created examination and credential.

Drane, J. "Should a Hospital Ethicist Have Clinical Experience?" *Hlth Progress* 66 (1985):60–63.

A philosopher by training, Drane answers the question in the title by demonstrating the dangers for institutions in which their clinical ethicists do not have extensive clinical experience. Physicians should be the ethical experts.

Fowler, M. "The Role of the Clinical Ethicist." *Heart and Lung* **15, no. 3 (1986):318–19.**

Optimally, the clinical ethicist has credentials as both a health care professional and a professional ethicist. Because this ideal is hard to meet, clinicians with some formal preparation in ethical theory or bioethicists with substantial clinical experience can become clinical ethicists.

Glover, J., D. Ozar, and D. Thomasma. "Teaching Ethics on Rounds: Ethicist as Teacher, Consultant and Decisionmaker." *Theor Med* **7 (1986):13–32.**

An early descriptive analysis of three potential roles for the hospital-based ethicist: decision-maker is a role that ethicists should never take; teacher is a natural, everyday role; and the consultant/ethicist raises questions to help learners learn.

Jonsen, A. "Can an Ethicist Be a Consultant?" In *Frontiers in Medical Ethics: Applications in a Medical Setting,* **by V. Abernethy. Cambridge, Mass.: Ballinger Press, 1980, 157–71.**

The first paper to explicitly address this question. Lucid, thoughtful, and clear, Jonsen's answer is "it depends — use a new casuistry, and be careful out there."

———. "Casuistry as Methodology in Clinical Ethics." *Theor Med* **12 (1991):295–307.**

"Casuistry is the exercise of prudential or practical reasoning in recognition of the relationship between maxims, circumstances and topics, as well as the relationship of paradigms to analogous cases."

Kass, E., J. Kirsner, T. Benedek, S. Peitzman, and J. Howell. "The Subspecialties of Internal Medicine: Case Studies." In *Grand Rounds: One Hundred Years of Internal Medicine,* **Edited by R. Maulitz and D. Long. University of Pennsylvania Press, 1988, 85–275.**

The development of infectious disease, gastroenterology, rheumatology, nephrology, and cardiology is traced by distinguished senior clinicians in each field.

La Puma, J. "Consultation Clinical Ethics: Issues and Questions in 27 Cases." *West J Med* 146 (1987):633–37.

In the first empirical study of an ethics consultant's cases, this paper identifies the questions asked and the issues perceived in each case and suggests key areas of consultation research for the future.

La Puma, J., and D. Schiedermayer. "Ethics Consultation: Skills, Roles and Training." *Ann Intern Med* 114 (1991):155–60.

Ethics consultants have expertise in the bedside identification, analysis, and resolution of ethical problems in patient care. Specialized training is needed to build the consultant's particular skills and roles.

——. "The Clinical Ethicist at the Bedside." *Theor Med* 12 (1991):141–49.

Three cases ground a more theoretical argument for the importance of the *sine qua non* of the clinical ethics consultant: going to the patient's bedside to obtain specific clinical and ethical information.

La Puma, J., D. Schiedermayer, S. Toulmin, S. Miles, and J. McAtee. "The Standard of Care: A Case Report and Ethical Analysis." *Ann Intern Med* 108 (1988):121–24.

Consultants must be clinicians who understand the technical aspects, legal implications, and motives behind requests for consultation.

Orr, R., and R. Moss. "The Family Physician and Ethics at the Bedside." *J Amer Brd Fam Pract* 6, no. 1 (1993):49–54.

The broad medical training, considerations of others, and interest in personal and social detail that characterize family medicine make the family physician well suited to train and consult in clinical ethics.

Pellegrino, E. "Ethics and the Moment of Clinical Truth." *JAMA* 239 (1978): 960–61, and E. Pellegrino. "Clinical Ethics — Biomedical Ethics at the Bedside." *JAMA* 260 (1988):837–39.

In two landmark commentaries, Pellegrino points out the need for faithfulness to the patient, attention to the details of the patient's illness, and careful, thoughtful weighing of empiric analyses to ethical questions.

——, M. Singer, and P. Singer. "Future Directions in Clinical Ethics." *J Clin Eth* 2, no. 1 (1991):5–9.
Six key areas in clinical ethics warrant special attention, including certification for ethics consultants. The authors predict that adequate clinical training will be central to certification.

Perkins, H. "Teaching Medical Ethics During Residency." *Acad Med* 64 (1989):262–66.
Resident physicians can develop the skills and knowledge base needed to identify and resolve the ethical dilemmas presented during training. Rotation on an ethics consultation service can be an important part of residency training.

Schiedermayer, D., J. La Puma, and S. Miles. "Ethics Consultations Masking Economic Dilemmas in Patient Care." *Arch Intern Med* 149 (1989):1303–5.
When the problem is money, ethics consultants are often asked to help resolve economic issues. Ethics consultants can act as patient advocates in these situations.

Shattuck, F. "Specialism, the Laboratory, and Practical Medicine." *Boston Med Surg* 136 (1987):613–17.
A classic, clear, and prescient analysis of the proper relationship between the cornerstone of medical practice (the laboratory and its research results) and physicians' natural inclination to want to know more (specialization).

Siegler, M. "Medical Consultation in the Context of the Physician–Patient Relationship." In *Responsibility in Health Care*, Edited by G. Agich. Dordrecht, Holland: D. Reidel Publishing Company, 1982, 141–62.
Voluntary, mutual, consensual, and noncoercive agreement among all concerned characterizes the ideal request for consultation.

The request for consultation is not a request for a primary consult-ant–patient relationship or a health care team–patient relationship, nor is it a referral. A consultant serves at the primary physician's invitation.

Skeel, J., and D. Self. "An Analysis of Ethics Consultation in the Clinical Setting." *Theor Med* 10 (1989):289–99.

There is risk associated with ethics consultation: value conflicts of interest for the ethicist, as well as questions regarding patient confidentiality and privacy. Such risks may, however, be outweighed by improved communication between patient and others.

Thomasma, D. "Medical Ethics Training: A Clinical Partner-ship." *J Med Education* 54 (1979):897–99.

A pioneering report of an institutionally supported, collaborative experiment. A university medical center and a veterans administration hospital cooperated to create an educational ethics consultation service.

————. "Medical Ethics: A Clinical Base." *Linacre Q* 49 (1982):266–76.

The author carefully analyzes three objections to clinical ethics (outside interference, inadequate theory, and nothing to offer), calling for a clinically based medical ethics.

————. "Why Philosophers Should Offer Ethics Consultations." *Theor Med* 12 (1991):129–40.

Philosophers offer the basic philosophical and cognitive abilities needed for ethics consultation, including "discovering the important hierarchy of values in a specific context." The author advocates certification for philosopher/consultants.

Wear, S. "The Irreducibly Clinical Character of Bioethics." *J Med Philos* 16 (1991):53–70.

Becoming competent in both clinical medicine and ethical analysis is a significant but necessary undertaking, especially for those ethicists interested in seeing patients.

Wiecha, J. "Ethics in Medicine: Are We Blind? In Support of Teaching Medical Ethics at the Bedside." *J Med Human* 12, no. 3 (1991):111–17.

A senior medical student makes a plea for bedside education in ethics, describing the case of a Jehovah's Witness who refused and then acceded to a transfusion.

SETTING UP PRACTICE

Agich, G. "Clinical Ethics: A Role Theoretic Look." *Soc Sci and Med* 30, no. 4 (1990):389–99.

Consulting, teaching, watching, and witnessing are differentiated. The first two roles comprise consultation practice; the last two roles are transitional states, which are necessary for the consultant to consult and teach.

Anzia, D., and J. La Puma. "Quality Care and Clinical Ethics." *QRB* 18 (1992):21–23.

Discrete, potentially measurable features of the consultation process are suggested. Reasonable, patient-centered, and clinician-centered measures of potential outcome are derived from the process.

Bermel, J. "Ethics Consultants: A Self-Portrait of Decisionmakers." *Hast Cent Rept* 15, no. 6 (1985):2.

A summary of 38 respondents' replies to a self-administered questionnaire distributed before the 1985 National Institutes of Health–University of California San Francisco invited conference on ethics consultation. The results of this survey are more fully reported in *Ethics Consultation in Health Care*.

Brennan, T. "Quality of Clinical Ethics Consultation." *QRB* 18 (1992):4–5.

Cross-fertilization between clinical ethics consultation and quality improvement can result in improved health care organizations.

Cranford, R. "The Neurologist as Ethics Consultant and as a Member of the Institutional Ethics Committee: The Neuroethicist." *Neurol Clin* 7, no. 4 (1989):697–713.

Neurologists are well suited to become ethics consultants, because many ethics cases concern patients who are cognitively impaired. Neurologists may be able to both clarify diagnostic data and teach committee members how to consider these data in an ethical analysis.

Fletcher, J. "Ethics Consultation Services: An Overview." *Biolaw* 2, no. 34 (1990): S339–47.

Consultation services should have discrete, clearly identified goals that have broad institutional sponsorship. An ethics consultation protocol should have the support of the institution's administration. Consultation should be available to all members of the health care team, but the attending physician should approve the request.

———. "Needed: A Broader View of Ethics Consultation." *QRB* 18 (1992):12–14.

Credentialing needs careful analysis. Members of the University of Virginia ethics consultation service have clinical privileges in ethics consultation and are covered by institutional liability insurance.

Frader, J. "Political and Interpersonal Aspects of Ethics Consultation." *Theor Med* 13 (1992):31–44.

A candid, especially thoughtful assessment of institutional and relational power and authority issues that may affect the consultant's opinion in a given case. Consultants should take responsibility for their actions and their consequences.

Goldman, L., T. Lee, and P. Rudd. "Ten Commandments for Effective Consultations." *Arch Intern Med* 143 (1983):1753–55.

Sensible, clear, commonsense guidelines for consultants. Although written for internists, ethics consultants should tap the wisdom of others who have been consulting a while, regardless of their cognitive fields of expertise.

Kapp, M. "Are Risk Management and Health Care Ethics Compatible?" *Persp Hlthcare Risk Management* 198, no. 4 (1991):2–7.

The short answer is "yes." Kapp tells how risk managers should consider confidentiality, privacy, record keeping, and institutional character, striving to protect patients and avoid lawsuit.

Lang, D. "The Case for Consultation." *Hlth Exec* **2, no. 4 (1987):40–43.**

An informal report of cases as seen by a community hospital consultant yields suggestions for accomplishing patient care goals by working with top management and within the existing administrative hierarchy.

La Puma, J. "Clinical Ethics, Mission and Vision; Practical Wisdom in Health Care." *Hosp and Hlth Serv Admin* **35 (1990):321–26.**

Top management must sponsor a clinical ethics program for it to succeed. Making clinical ethics an explicit part of the institutional mission is an appropriate, clear message to give staff, patients, and families.

———, and E. Priest. "Medical Staff Privileges for Ethics Consultants: An Institutional Model." *QRB* **18, no. 1 (1992):17–20.**

One process of obtaining consulting privileges in clinical ethics is reviewed and critiqued, including the needed evaluation and monitoring of these privileges.

Miles, S., L. Lane, J. Bickel, R. Walker, and C. Cassel. "Medical Ethics Education: Coming of Age." *Acad Med* **64, no. 12 (1989):705–14.**

One hundred references suggest the scope of this review. The authors identify the ethics training that students and residents must have to work as clinicians and practitioners. A page-long, referenced table of content areas in medical ethics is especially helpful.

Nelson, S. "Liability Issues Increasing Ethics Consultations." *Hospitals* **(May 5, 1987):80–84.**

Institutions may use ethics consultations to reduce their legal risk, although the primary purpose of consultation is to assist in decision-making, resolve disagreements, and help in managing difficult patient cases.

1993 Accreditation Manual for Hospitals, Volume 1, Standards.
Oakbrook Terrace, Ill.: Joint Commission on the Accreditation of
Health Care Organizations, 1992.
   The JCAHO requires members to have a mechanism for assist-
ing in "the resolution of moral dilemmas in patient care." Ethics
consultants can help institutions meet this requirement.

O'Leary, D. "Accreditation in the Quality Improvement Mold – A
Vision for Tomorrow." QRB 17, no. 2 (1991):72–77.
   The continuous quality improvement (CQI) process has gathered momentum in health care and is an ongoing effort to improve
performance by monitoring and evaluating empirical data about key
processes and outcomes. The processes and outcomes of ethics
consultation could certainly fit in such a model.

Scofield, G. "The Problems of the Impaired Clinical Ethicist."
QRB 18 (1992):26–32.
   The author hypothesizes that ethics consultants, like other
highly stressed health professionals, may become impaired, and the
author warns of potential problems in the quality of care delivered by
impaired consultants.

Self, D., and J. Skeel. "Professional Liability (Malpractice) Coverage of Humanist Scholars Functioning as Clinical Medical
Ethicists." J Med Hum and Bioeth 9, no. 2 (1988):101–9.
   Only 9 clinical ethicists with educational backgrounds in philosophy or religion of the 101 responding clinical ethicists reported
that they regularly wrote in the medical record, although 29 were
certain that they were covered by professional liability insurance.
Few reported making recommendations in patient care.

Siegler, M. "Defining the Goals of Ethics Consultations: A Necessary Step for Improving Quality." QRB 18 (1992):15–16.
   More empiric data and datasets are needed to validate the
efficacy and utility of ethics consultations. These data should first
describe desirable outcomes for consultation and then evaluate
whether consultations produce those outcomes.

Volpintesta, and J. Schecter. "Ethics Consultants Need Doctors' Support." *Hast Cent Rept* 16, no. 4 (1986):48.

Two physicians note that many physicians do not recognize medical ethics as a priority, although they should. They also note that ethics consultants do not often venture into the trenches of patient care and that they should.

Whiteneck, M. "Integrating Ethics With Quality Assurance in Long Term Care." *QRB* 14, no. 3 (1988):138–43.

In nursing homes and retirement centers, ethical problems are inseparable from quality improvement problems. Improving quality assurance processes may help resolve ethical problems.

CONSULTANTS AND COMMITTEES

Agich, G., and S. Youngner. "For Experts Only? Access to Hospital Ethics Committees." *Hast Cent Rept* 21, no. 5 (1991):17–25.

Consultation should be carried out by individual consultants instead of small consultation teams. Consultants and committees should be complementary, not competitive.

Anderek, W. "Development of a Hospital Ethics Committee: Lessons From Five Years of Case Consultations." *Cambridge Q of Hlthcare Ethics* 1, no. 1 (1992):41–50.

Forty-four consultation requests in an urban community hospital are reported; 41 of these questions regard foregoing life-sustaining treatment. Limiting consultation requests to those from the attending physician seemed to increase the credibility of the committee and promote acceptance of its recommendations.

Annas, G. "Ethics Committees: From Ethical Comfort to Ethical Cover." *Hast Cent Rept* 21, no. 3 (1991):18–21.

Committees that consult should avoid becoming bureaucratic, making legal pronouncements and acting as quasi-judicial bodies, a task for which they are untrained. In individual case consultation, ethics consultants are replacing ethics committees.

Brennan, T. "Ethics Committees and Decisions to Limit Care: The Experience at the Massachusetts General Hospital." JAMA 260 (1988):803–7.

A large retrospective review of requests for ethics committee consultation that shows an increase in requests over time. The author divides the consultations into categories, the largest of which includes requests to forgo life-sustaining treatment.

Carter, B. "Medical Ethics Committee — A Survey of Army Hospitals." *Military Hospitals* 153 (1988):426–29.

Of 37 physician administrators in army health care institutions, 33 returned questionnaires. The survey showed that 25 hospitals already had ethics committees and that 27 institutions believed that such committees should have a consultative role.

Caws, P. "Committees and Consensus: How Many Heads Are Better Than One?" *J Med and Philos* 16, no. 4 (1991):375–91.

Caws is skeptical about the wisdom of committee decision-making, especially about clinical cases.

Cranford, R., and J. Roberts. "Biomedical Ethics Committees." *Primary Care* 13, no. 2 (1986):327–41.

Consultation is the committee function given to the greatest potential for controversy; still, it may have benefits, especially for committee members who wish to learn about medical ethics.

Fleetwood, J., R. Arnold, and R. Baron. "Giving Answers or Raising Questions?: The Problematic Role of Institutional Ethics Committees." *J Med Ethics* 15 (1989):137–42.

The authors point out that committees are better suited to examine ethical issues than to see individual patients.

Fletcher, J. "The Bioethics Movement and Hospital Ethics Committees." *Maryland Law Review* 50, no. 3 (1991):859–88.

The ethics consultant derives institutional accountability from his or her membership in the ethics committee. The committee should not act as a quasi-judicial body, but as a sounding board and support mechanism for the consultant.

Fletcher, J. "Ethics Committees and Due Process." *Law, Med and Hlth Care* 21 (1993); in press.

Referred to in a Spring 1993 *Newsletter of the Society for Bioethics Consultation*, this piece advocates a subgroup of ethics committee members as consultants, using subspecialists as needed.

Fost, N., and R. Cranford. "Hospital Ethics Committees: Administrative Aspects." JAMA 253 (1985):2687–92.

A classic paper that reviews the different ways committees can function. The authors favor a committee that prospectively reviews cases on an optional/optional format: the consultation is optional and following the committee's recommendations is also optional rather than mandatory.

Freedman, B. "One Philosopher's Experience on an Ethics Committee." *Hast Cent Rept* 11, no. 2 (1981):20–22.

Musings about a year's experience on a newly formed ethics consultation service in a Canadian teaching hospital: a bioethicist finds a new language and a new culture, and works to understand it.

Gramelspacher, G. "Institutional Ethics Committees and Case Consultation: Is There a Role?" *Issues Law and Med* 7, no. 1 (1991):73–82.

Committees that consult must establish formal, deliberate procedures for consulting and a formal, rigorous prospective evaluation mechanism. Evaluation should have two, distinguishable spheres: process and content.

Grodin, M., W. Markley, and A. McDonald. "Use of an Institutional Ethics Team on a Pediatric Service." QRB 11 (1985):16–19.

The authors review retrospectively collected data on a large number of pediatric cases seen by an ethics committee consultation subcommittee. Most cases concerned end-of-life care issues.

Hoffman, D. "Does Legislating Hospital Ethics Committees Make a Difference? A Study of Hospital Ethics Committees in Maryland, the District of Columbia, and Virginia." *Law, Med and Hlth Care* 19, nos. 1–2 (1991):106–33.

A careful, thoughtful, multifaceted four-phase study. Committee demographics, education, purposes, procedures, sociological interactions, and influences are reported. Ten percent of 60 committees that had performed consultations had done more than 16 in the past year.

Kliegman, R., M. Mahowald, and S. Youngner. "In Our Best Interests: Experience and Workings of an Ethics Review Committee." J Peds 108, no. 2 (1986):178–88.

A retrospective review of 11 pediatric consultations requested over 15 months, with a detailing of the committee's basic assumptions, membership, procedures, and operative principles, including the need for collaboration and rational analysis.

La Puma, J., C. Darling, C. Stocking, and K. Schiller. "A Perinatal Ethics Committee on Abortion: Process and Outcome in 31 Cases." J Clin Eth 3, no. 3 (1992):196–203.

A one-year study of a mandatory prospective perinatal ethics committee (PEC) on abortion. Thirty-one requests (mean gestation 18.3 weeks, range 6–23) were submitted and approved in a mean of 4.6 days (range 1–15). Of 377 committee interactions, 70 percent concerned the regulatory process; 63 percent of regulatory actions concerned procedures, documentation, or policy relevant to the case.

La Puma, J. and S. Toulmin. "Ethics Consultants and Ethics Committees." Arch Intern Med 149 (1989):1109–12.

Ethics consultants and ethics committees can be complementary. Consultants should see patients and give practical help to requesting clinicians; committees should do policy work and education.

Lo, B. "Behind Closed Doors: Promises and Pitfalls of Ethics Committees." N Engl J Med 317 (1987):46–50.

Ethics committees have pros and cons, almost all of which have yet to be empirically evaluated. Safeguards are needed against groupthink and secondhand information.

Macklin, R. "The Inner Workings of an Ethics Committee: Latest Battle over Jehovah's Witnesses." Hast Cent Rpt 18, no. 2 (1988):15–20.

Ethics committees can use specific cases to help them formulate policies.

Mahowald, M. "Baby Doe Committees: A Critical Evaluation." Clin Perinatology 15, no. 4 (1988):789–800.
No ethical dilemma at all is usually found in cases presented to Baby Doe committees; nevertheless, committee members can learn from each other how to facilitate and optimize decision making.

———. "Hospital Ethics Committees: Diverse and Problematic." HEC Forum 1 (1989):237–46.
Having participated in six ethics committees in less than 12 years, the author is skeptical about their helpfulness to patients and their ability to debate philosophical issues.

Michaels, R., and T. Oliver. "Human Rights Consultation: A 12-Year Experience of a Pediatric Bioethics Committee." Peds 78, no. 4 (1986): 566–72.
An important retrospective review of 48 human rights consultations over 12 years; 41 consultations were for children under age 2, most of whom had congenital malformations. A physician–nonphysician team saw most of the patients. In 27 cases, the advisability of mechanical ventilation was the reason for consultation.

Miles, S. "New Business for Ethics Committees." HEC Forum 4, no. 2 (1992):97–102.
Decisions to transfer medically indigent patients, financial incentives for physicians' decisions, conflicts of interests in referrals, and economically restricted care are clinical, economic, and ethical issues. Hospital ethics committees should take on these issues and offer suggestions for policy decisions.

Moreno, J. "What Means This Consensus? Ethics Committees and Philosophic Tradition." J Clin Eth 1, no. 1 (1990):38–43, and Gregory, D. "Consensus: Real or Imaginary." J Clin Eth 1, no. 1 (1990):43–44, and Shenk, I. "Consensus – The Measure of Ethical Permissibility: A Response to Jonathan Moreno." J Clin Eth 1, no. 1 (1990):45.

Because everyone agrees, does that make it right? Three views, as the answer to this question pertains to ethics committees that debate moral issues in a particular patient's care.

Ross, J. "Case Consultation: The Committee or the Clinical Consultant?" *HEC Forum* 2, no. 5 (1990):289–98.
Ross argues that individual consultants cannot match the multi-disciplinary breadth that ethics committees can muster. Moreover, ethics committees as a whole can offer conceptual advice about how to handle similar cases to practitioners who appear before them.

Shapiro, R., and R. Barthel. "Infant Care Committees: An Effective Approach to the Baby Doe Dilemma?" *Hast Law J* 37, no. 5 (1986):827–62.
Baby Doe squads have outlived their usefulness. Instead of being content to settle for technical and legal solutions to ethical problems, hospitals can empower infant care review committees to act clinically to help infants, parents, and providers work through ethical problems.

Siegler, M. "Ethics Committees: Decisions by Bureaucracy." *Hast Cent Rept* 16, no. 3 (1986):22–24.
An argument that ethics committees should not perform consultations that intrude on the doctor–patient relationship, but should only play an educational and policy-making role.

Singer, P., E. Pellegrino, and M. Siegler. "Ethics Committees and Consultants." *J Clin Eth* 1, no. 4 (1990):263–67.
The central goal of consultation is to improve patient care and patient outcomes; consultations are difficult to evaluate because the outcomes of interest have not been clearly identified. Insufficient data exists to establish the superiority of any one model of performing a consultation.

Swenson, M., and R. Miller. "Ethics Case Review in Health Care Institutions: Committees, Consultants, or Teams?" *Arch Intern Med* 152, no. 4 (1992):694–97.

The authors postulate advantages and disadvantages to both ethics committees and consultants. Consultations should be performed by a consultative team that has a separate identity from the committee.

West, M., and J. Gibson. "Facilitating Medical Ethics Case Review: What Ethics Committees Can Learn From Mediation and Facilitation Techniques." *Cambridge Q Hlthcare Eth* **1 (1992):63–74.**
Training in mediation and facilitation is important in consultation. Committee consultants should follow up after each consultation to provide committee members with outcome data and to address other ethical issues that have arisen.

Wolf, S. "Ethics Committees and Due Process: Nesting Rights in a Community of Caring." *Maryland Law Review* **50, no. 3 (1991):798–858.**
Committees that consult must engage in a due, public process of consideration and decision making. A quasi-judicial role for consultative committees is needed, is appropriate, and should be patient-centered, as patients require strong advocacy.

Youngner, S., C. Coulton, B. Juknialis, and D. Jackson. "Patients' Attitudes Toward Hospital Ethics Committees." *Law, Med and Hlth Care* **12, no. 1 (1984):21–25.**
An important documentation of patient views: although 76 percent of the 120 healthy outpatient respondents thought ethics committees could be useful in hospitals, only 12 percent felt that an ethics committee should "make the final decision."

BOOKS ON CONSULTATION

Ackerman, T., G. Graber, C. Reynolds, and D. Thomasma, eds. *Clinical Medical Ethics: Exploration and Assessment.* **Lanham, Md.: University Press of America, 1987.**
The proceedings of a 1982 conference, this collection of essays focuses on the philosophical credibility of ethics consultation and

proposes several different models for teaching clinical ethics, including a bedside model.

Cranford, R., and A. Doudera, eds. *Institutional Ethics Committees and Health Care Decision Making.* Ann Arbor: Health Administration Press, 1984.

One of the first books on committees and consultants. Its chapters reflect the serious consideration that ethics committees give to their proper roles, duties, and obligations.

Culver, C, ed. *Ethics at the Bedside.* Hanover, N.H.: University of New England Press, 1990.

Personal stories and public confessions comprise this book written for the public. Several esteemed bioethicists write of their most interesting or difficult patients, including a consultant's dying mother-in-law, for whom the consultant negotiated adequate morphine dosages.

Fletcher, J., N. Quist, and A. Jonsen, eds. *Ethics Consultation in Health Care.* Ann Arbor: Health Administration Press, 1989.

The results of a 1985 symposium on ethics consultation, with a very good introduction and an excellent chapter on the nature of the clinical role. The work otherwise assumes a theoretical orientation.

Fry-Revere, S. *The Accountability of Bioethics Committees and Consultants.* Frederick, Md.: University Publishing, 1992.

A philosophical and regulatory book, suggesting oversight of ethics consultation by institutional ethics committees. Legal arguments for the position are made, embracing nonclinicians.

Jonsen, A., M. Siegler, and W. Winslade. *Clinical Ethics: A Practical Approach to Ethical Decisions in Clinical Medicine.* 3d ed. New York: McGraw-Hill, Health Professions Division, 1992.

A practical book whose major contribution is the definition of clinical ethics as the identification and resolution of moral issues in patient care. The authors describe a four-point model of decision making: medical indications, patient preferences, quality of life, and socioeconomic factors.

Young, E. *Alpha and Omega: Ethics at the Frontiers of Life and Death.* Reading, MA: Addison-Wesley, 1989.

Contains many accounts of ethics consultations, as seen by a clinically sensitive, well-informed chaplain who functions as a clinical ethicist and who is insightful about patient cases.

SPECIAL REFERENCES FOR ILLUSTRATIVE CASES

Drane, J. "Competency to Give an Informed Consent: A Model for Making Clinical Assessments." JAMA 252 (1984):925–27.

As in Victor Adamavich's case, criteria for clinical decision-making capacity need not be unyielding but may be adjusted along a sliding scale with the severity of illness. Without such a scale, the goals of patient autonomy and patient medical improvement may oppose one another, to the patient's disadvantage.

Jonsen, A., M. Siegler, and W. Winslade. *Clinical Ethics: A Practical Approach to Ethical Decisions in Clinical Medicine.* 3d ed. New York: McGraw-Hill, Health Professions Division, 1992.

The discussion of considerations when treating patients with unusual belief systems is clinically sensitive; this book was quoted in the case of Wilma Shell.

Notes

CHAPTER 1

1. C. Allen et al., "A Randomized Controlled Clinical Trial of a Geriatric Consultation Team—Compliance with Recommendations," *JAMA* 255 (1986):2617–21.
2. G. Merli and H. Wirtz, "The Medical Consultant," *Med Clin North Amer* 71 (1987):353–55.
3. L. Kass, *Toward a More Natural Science* (New York: The Free Press, 1985).
4. J. La Puma et al., "An Ethics Consultation Service in a Teaching Hospital: Utilization and Evaluation," *JAMA* 260 (1988):808–11.
5. J. La Puma et al., "Community Hospital Ethics Consultation: Evaluation and Comparison with a University Hospital Service," *Amer J Med* 92 (1992):346–351.
6. J. La Puma et al., "A Perinatal Ethics Committee on Abortion: Process and Outcome in 31 Cases," *J Clin Eth* 3 (1992):196–203.
7. D. Anzia and J. La Puma, "Quality Care and Clinical Ethics," *QRB* 18, no. 1 (1992):21–23.

CHAPTER 2

1. H. Perkins and B. Saathoff, "Impact of Medical Ethics Consultations on Physicians: An Exploratory Study," *Amer J Med* 85 (1988):761–65.
2. J. La Puma et al., "Community Hospital Ethics Consultation: Evaluation and Comparison With a University Hospital Service," *Amer J Med* 92 (1992): 346–51.
3. J. La Puma and D. Schiedermayer, "Ethics Consultation: Skills, Roles and Training," *Ann Intern Med* 114 (1991):155–60.
4. R. Orr and C. Moon, "Effectiveness of an Ethics Consultation Service," *J Fam Pract* 36, no. 1 (1993):49–53.

5. M. Grodin, W. Markley, and A. McDonald, "Use of an Institutional Ethics Team on a Pediatric Service," QRB 11 (1985):16–19.
6. R. Michaels and T. Oliver, "Human Rights Consultation: A 12-year Experience of a Pediatric Bioethics Committee," Pediatrics 78, no. 4 (1986):566–72.
7. T. Brennan, "Ethics Committees and Decisions to Limit Care: The Experience at the Massachusetts General Hospital," JAMA 260 (1988):803–7.
8. S. Wolf, "Ethics Committees and Due Process: Nesting Rights in a Community of Caring," Maryland Law Review 50, no. 3 (1991):798–858.
9. J. La Puma et al., "An Ethics Consultation Service in a Teaching Hospital: Utilization and Evaluation," JAMA 260 (1988):808–11.
10. P. Rudd, "Problems in Consultation Medicine: The Generalist's Reply," J Genl Intern Med 3 (1988):592–95.
11. L. Goldman, T. Lee, and P. Rudd, "Ten Commandments for Effective Consultations," Arch Intern Med 143 (1983):1753–55.
12. J. Drane, "Hiring a Hospital Ethicist," in J. Fletcher, N. Quist, and A. Jonsen, eds., Ethics Consultation in Health Care (Ann Arbor: Health Administration Press, 1989), 117 – 34.

CHAPTER 3

1. J. La Puma et al., "Prospective Evaluation of an Ethics Consultation Service," Clin Res 35, no. 2 (1987):748A.
2. A. Owens, "How Much Did Your Earnings Grow Last Year?" Medical Economics (September 5, 1988):159–80.
3. Hays and Associates, "Evaluation of Clinical Ethics Position" (Personal communication from Robin Fell to John La Puma, January 1992).
4. The 1992 Accreditation Manual for Hospitals (Chicago: The Joint Commission on the Accreditation of Healthcare Organizations, 1989).
5. J. La Puma and E. Priest, "Medical Staff Privileges for Ethics Consultants: An Institutional Model," QRB 18 (1992):17–20.
6. P. Singer, S. Miles, and M. Siegler, "Computer Searching of the Medical Ethics Literature," J Clin Eth 1, no. 3 (1990):195–98.

7. "A Survey of Ethics Consultants — Statistical Analysis" (Prepared for Dr. John Fletcher, National Institutes of Health, September 1985).

8. H. Perkins and B. Saathoff, "Impact of Medical Ethics Consultations on Physicians: An Exploratory Study," *Amer J Med* 85 (1988):761–65.

9. R. Orr, "Evaluation of a New Ethics Consultation Service" (Presented at the Fourth Annual Mrs. John C. McClean Conference on Clinical Medical Ethics and Patient Care, The University of Chicago, 19 October 1991).

10. J. La Puma, "Clinical Ethics, Mission and Vision; Practical Wisdom in Health Care," *Hosp and Health Serv Admin* 35 (1990):321–26.

11. J. La Puma, "Researching For-Profit Research: The Obligations of Hospital Ethicists," *Clin Res* 37, no. 4 (1989):569–73.

12. T. Muldary, *Burnout and Health Professionals: Manifestations and Management* (Norwalk, Conn.: Appleton Century Crofts, 1983).

13. J. Pfifferling, *The Impaired Physician: An Overview* (Chapel Hill, N.C.: Center for the Well-Being of Health Professionals, 1980), 4.

CHAPTER 4

1. S. Miles, "Informed Demand for Nonbeneficial Medical Treatment," *N Engl J Med* 325 (1991):512–15.

2. The National Commission for the Protection of Human Subjects of Biomedical and Behavioral Research, *The Belmont Report: Ethical Principles and Guidelines for the Protection of Human Subjects of Research* (Washington, D.C.: U.S. Government Printing Office, 1978), DHEW pub. no. (OS) 78-0012, 78-0013, and 78-0014.

3. *The 1992 Accreditation Manual for Hospitals* (Chicago: The Joint Commission on the Accreditation of Healthcare Organizations, 1989).

4. H. Larkin, "Liability Fears Interfering With Clinical Decisions, Physicians Say," *Amer Med News,* 22/29 April 1991, 11.

5. *Wickline v. California,* 192 Cal. App. 3d 1630, 239 Cal. Rptr 810 (1986).

6. "AMA/Specialty Society Medical Liability Project," *Risk Management Principles and Commentaries for the Medical Office.* (Chicago: The American Medical Association, 1990).

7. M. Kapp, "Are Risk Management and Health Care Ethics Compatible?" *Perspectives in Healthcare Risk Management* (Winter 1991):2–7.

Index